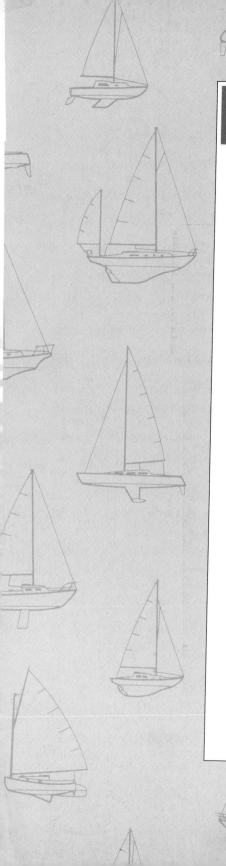

THE INTERNATIONAL MARINE SAILBOAT LIBRARY

SAILBOAT REFINISHING

DON CASEY

INTERNATIONAL MARINE

CAMDEN, MAINE

CONTENTS

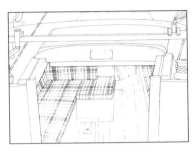

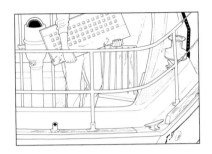

Introduction   4

The Basics   7

Understanding Paints and Other Marine Coatings   8

Which Brand Is the Best? • Local Knowledge • Product Guide

Good Results from Good Tools   22

Judging Brush Quality • The Right Brush for the Job • Cleaning Technique • Wrapping the Bristles • Roller Covers • Cage-Type Roller Handle • Cutting Roller Covers for Specific Needs • Sandpaper Types and Uses • Disk Sander • Sanding Block • Orbital Sander • Folding Sandpaper for Hand Sanding • Scrapers • Sharpening a Scraper • Rags • Disposable Coveralls and Cap • Gloves, Goggles, and Respirator

Preparation   33

Removing Trim and Hardware • Cleaning • Degreasing • Removing Any Trace of Silicone • Checking the Old Paint with Solvent • Checking the Old Paint with Tape • Using Chemical Stripper • Power Sanding with a Disk Sander • Using a Palm Sander • Hand Sanding • Cleaning Raw Wood After Sanding • Cleaning Finished Surfaces • Wetting Down Around the Paint Area

Inside the Cabin   45

Ready to Paint   46

Pouring Paint and Resealing the Container • Using a Paint Filter • Thinning

Painting   49

Brushing Techniques • Using a Paint Roller • Tipping for a Smoother Finish • Keeping Tools and Paint Fresh

Plastic Laminates   53

Checking for Adhesion of the Old Laminate • Disk Sanding the Surface • Making a Paper Pattern • Cutting the New Laminate • Applying the Contact Cement • Keeping the Glue-Coated Surfaces Apart While Positioning • Removing the Separator • Rolling a Good Bond • Trimming with a Router or a File • Replacing the Trim

Wood Finishes   63

Oiling Wood Trim   64

Scrubbing Teak • Lightening the Color • Using a Two-Part Teak Cleaner • Applying Teak Oil • Wiping Interior Wood Surfaces with Lemon Oil

Sealers   68

Preparing Old Wood • Applying a Sealer

Varnishing: Preparation   69

Stripping Old Varnish • Bleaching Raw Wood • Surface Preparation

Varnishing: The Initial Coats   75

When to Varnish • Bubbles—the Nemesis • Brushing Technique • Sanding Between Coats • Keeping the Surface Dust-Free • The Third and Fourth Coats

"Laying On" the Finish Coats   79

The Last Coat • Maintaining a Varnished Surface

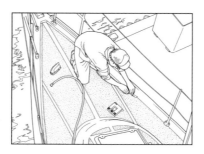

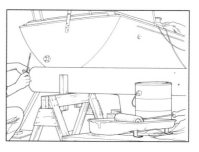

Below the Waterline 83

Antifouling Bottom Coatings 84

Preparing the Bottom for Recoating • Using Peel-Type Stripper • Fairing and Minor Blister Repair • Mixing Bottom Paint • Roller Application • Racing Application • Burnishing Antifouling Coatings • Applying Cuprous Resin • Props, Zincs, and Transducers

Bootstripe 94

Finding the Waterline • Positioning the Bootstripe • Masking the Stripe • Painting the Bootstripe

Anti-Blister Coating 98

What Causes Blisters? • Determining the Appropriate Treatment • Drying Out • Filling Blisters • Applying an Epoxy Barrier Coat

Topsides and Deck 103

Gelcoat Repair 104

Opening a Scratch for Repair • Gouges and Other Damage Repairs • Gelcoat Choices • Color Matching • Catalyzing • Spreading Gelcoat Paste • Applying Gelcoat with Spray • Applying Gelcoat with Brush • Applying Gelcoat with Roller • Sanding and Polishing Gelcoat Repairs

Two-Part Linear Polyurethane 112

Preparing the Surface • Checking for Porosity • Surface Crazing • Epoxy Primer • Mixing and Thinning Polyurethane Paint • Testing Flow-Out • Rolling Polyurethane (Light Colors Only) • The Roll-and-Tip Method (All Colors) • Wet Sanding Between Coats • Removing Sanding Scum • Getting a Mirror Finish

Refinishing the Deck 120

Dealing with Nonskid • Surface Preparation • Limiting Wet Edges to One • Painting Molded Nonskid Surfaces

Nonskid Overlay 125

Preparing the Surface • Cutting Patterns • Cutting the Overlay • Applying the Overlay

Finishing Touches 129

Refinishing the Mast 130

Graphics 132

Designing Custom Graphics • Laying Out Vinyl Graphics • Dealing with a Large Appliqué • Applying Vinyl Graphics

Index 138
Copyright page 142

INTRODUCTION

Of all the improvements that can be made to a boat showing the effects of a few seasons of use, none will have a more dramatic impact than refinishing. And few boat tasks are easier. This is a combination forged in Valhalla.

Exposure to the wondrous powers of paint began for most of us with a yellow and green box of crayons. More recent experience is likely to involve rollers and walls. Almost everyone has some painting experience. Whether your training is extensive or limited, if you select the right product and take a deliberate and careful approach to applying it to your boat, you are almost certain to be happy with the results.

The most satisfying result of doing your own refinishing used to be the amount of money saved. Unfortunately the quality of most self-applied marine coatings was somewhat less satisfying—often characterized as "good enough." Today the savings are even more impressive, but the biggest change is in the quality of the finish. Significant technological advances in paints and varnishes in recent years have sharply reduced the craftsmanship required to achieve "professional" results. New products have been engineered for amateur application, and the best of these have flow characteristics that result in finishes that are nothing short of spectacular.

Today's boatowner-applied paint jobs look far better than yard-applied coatings of only a few years back. Of course the improvements in technology have benefited the professional painter as well, but the flow characteristics of this new generation of paints are to a great extent independent of the hand holding the brush, meaning that a motivated amateur can get results that are distinguishable from a professional job only in a close side-by-side comparison. From the dock there will be no discernible difference.

Advances in marine varnish have been less revolutionary but still significant. Flow characteristics have been improved to the point that the foot-deep look of professionally maintained brightwork can be duplicated by the amateur. Improved durability and the addition of sun-screening agents extend the life of exposed varnish and reduce the work required to maintain the coating.

Another technological advance that directly benefits the do-it-yourself boat painter is the expansion of CAD/CAM (Computer Assisted Design/Computer Assisted Manufacturing) technology into boat graphics and lettering. Computer-generated vinyl appliqués are widely available today at a fraction of the cost of having similar lettering and graphics painted on. Lettering the stern of a boat in virtually any style imaginable is hardly more difficult now than putting a peel-and-stick label on an envelope. And the equally uncomplicated application of colorful graphics to the sides of a hull can transform an ordinary boat into a real attention-getter.

Bottom paints have also changed in recent years, although not necessarily for the better. For almost two decades, tin-based bottom paints were king, but while their multi-year protection was good for boatowners, the toxins they contained were bad for the marine environment. In 1989, tin-based bottom paints were banned in the United States (except for use on aluminum hulls), and paint manufacturers simply dropped back to the less-effective copper products they had been manufacturing since the sixties. These provide good antifouling protection for a single season and, in areas where boats stay in the water year-round, the better bottom paints maintain a degree of protection into the second year. None, however, are true multi-year coatings. Some "permanent" antifouling treatments are marketed, but none of these technologies has yet matured, and none of the permanent treatments is effective against grassy growth.

While product improvements have made it much easier to get professional results, the sheer number of products now offered add a significant complication to most refinishing projects. Gone are the days when boat paint was synonymous with enamel, when the choice among two or three brand names depended mostly on the colors available, and when a can of mineral spirits was the only other item required, serving as thinner, surface wipe, and for clean-up. The paint shelf of the past has been replaced by a paint department. Today's chandleries stock hundreds of marine coatings and dozens of coating "systems." A catalog from a large mail-order marine supplier will have 50 or more pages of paints and related products.

Think of this book as a tool, a set of tools really—like a set of socket wrenches. The three sections that make up Chapter 1 are like the ratchet and handles and extensions—the parts of the set you need for every job. The rest of the book is the array of sockets; for now you may only need the one or two that fit the job at hand, but the time will come when you need the others. When you do, they will be close at hand.

Whether you are simply looking for the best way to restore that warm, golden glow to long-neglected teak trim or you plan to refinish the boat from truck to keel, the instructions assembled in this guide are certain to save you time, money, and perhaps grief.

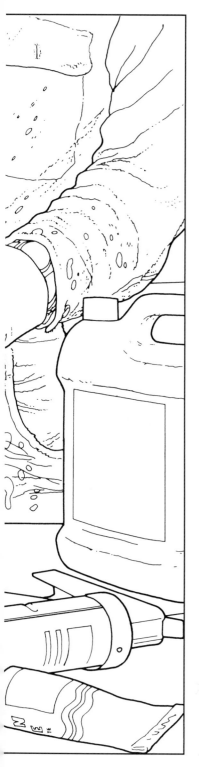

THE BASICS

Good results depend as much on selecting the right product as on application technique. To help you choose wisely, this initial chapter contains use and application information for common marine coatings and systems. Also included is the life expectancy of the resulting finish and the safety precautions, if any, that are required.

Another essential ingredient in achieving the best possible finish is good tools. Good-quality tools almost always allow you to do the job better and get it done quicker as well. The cost difference between a poor-quality brush and a top-quality one is just a few dollars, and the difference between a cheap roller cover and a good one even less, so there is little reason to compromise. For a first-class finish, select only the best painting tools. The second part of this chapter shows you how to choose the right tools, how to use them, and how to maintain them.

The third requirement common to all refinishing jobs is good preparation. While different coatings call for different preparation schedules, many of the specific steps are the same. Labeling and detailing those steps in a single location saves a great deal of unnecessary repetition. This part of the chapter is, in effect, an illustrated glossary applicable to the refinishing projects individually detailed in the remainder of the guide.

No matter what refinishing project you have in mind, you need the information contained in this first chapter. Don't skip over it. Most of it will not be repeated, and a good grasp of the basics is essential to achieving satisfactory results.

UNDERSTANDING PAINTS AND OTHER MARINE COATINGS

Faced with hundreds of different products, each one claiming to be the best, how do you make a selection? The process is significantly simplified if you know the class of product most appropriate for the refinishing job you have in mind.

Marine coatings are invariably formulated for a specific purpose—e.g., providing a hard, clear protective coating for wood, giving a high-gloss finish to dull gelcoat, or discouraging growth on the underwater portions of a boat. Any product on the shelf intended for your purpose will do the job, but not all will do it equally well. Performance is often dependent upon a key ingredient—without chili pepper, it just ain't Mexican food.

It is this key ingredient that gives a coating its defining characteristics—long life, high gloss, abrasion resistance, ease of application, or whatever. Since every paint manufacturer starts with the same basic ingredients, all the products in the category defined by that ingredient exhibit similar qualities regardless of the manufacturer.

That is not to say there aren't differences between brands—there are—but a difference in the recipe doesn't stop it from being an enchilada. If you want the longest-life paint, every manufacturer will recommend their two-part linear polyurethane. Likewise, if you want to oil your teak without darkening it, you will hear tung oil mentioned repeatedly.

What follows is an illustrated list of the various classes of marine coatings and related products (such as thinners). With few exceptions, all the paints and varnishes and sealants on the chandlery shelves fall into one of these categories, and you should be able to determine whether or not a particular class of product—and, by extension, a specific product brand—will satisfy your refinishing requirements.

WHICH BRAND IS THE BEST?

Perhaps you're wondering why not just cut to the chase and recommend products by brand name. After all, if there are differences between brands, then one brand must be better than the others, right?

It depends on what you're evaluating. For example, one manufacturer may formulate a paint that outlasts its competitors by 20 percent, but perhaps the extra durability comes at the expense of flow characteristics. Which is more important to you, a glassy finish or an extra season of durability?

It gets worse. The paint or varnish that seems to have them all beat in Connecticut may well lose its composure under the relentless sun of South Florida. In fact, some products carrying the same brand name are formulated differently for use in different parts of the country. Even if the formula isn't supposed to be different, the actual product often varies from batch to batch—chemical suppliers change, machinery fails, operators drift off. It's paint, not pharmaceuticals.

Still, some brands are undoubtedly better than others, and consumer boating magazines regularly run comparative tests of marine coatings. Such evaluations can be helpful in selecting a particular brand, but don't be surprised if the results vary between publications, or if this year's test results differ from those of only a couple of years ago. There are just too many variables—surface preparation, application, geographic location, weather patterns, boat use, water salinity, even evaluation criteria.

Don't count on any selection help from newsstand boating magazines. You may encounter a product "roundup" in a commercial publication, but don't expect to find any "let-the-chips-fall" test results. Rare is the boating magazine that will risk alienating potential advertisers by publishing negative results.

LOCAL KNOWLEDGE

So how do you make a selection? Your best source will often be local knowledge. If you ask other boatowners in your area what bottom paint they use, one brand name is likely to come up more often than others. If you see an old boat with a topside finish you admire, find out what the finish is and if it was owner-applied. If you hear praise for several different varnishes, get each advocate to show you his brightwork and ask the hard questions: How long has it been on? Always exposed? How many coats? How long between coats? You will know quickly enough precisely which product to choose and what to expect from it.

PRODUCT GUIDE

Marine paints and other boat refinishing products are constantly changing. New technologies provide continuing opportunities for tougher, smoother coatings. Environmental pressures lead to the elimination of specific ingredients or entire products. Products from other arenas find their way into marine use. (An example of the latter is the widespread use in Europe of a diaper-rash cream containing zinc oxide in place of antifouling paint.) In spite of this flux, most of the refinishing products on chandlery shelves have been around for years, some for decades. You are likely to find yourself choosing products that have a long history of marine use. Having a basic understanding of each of these products by class will help you select the specific product best suited to your individual needs.

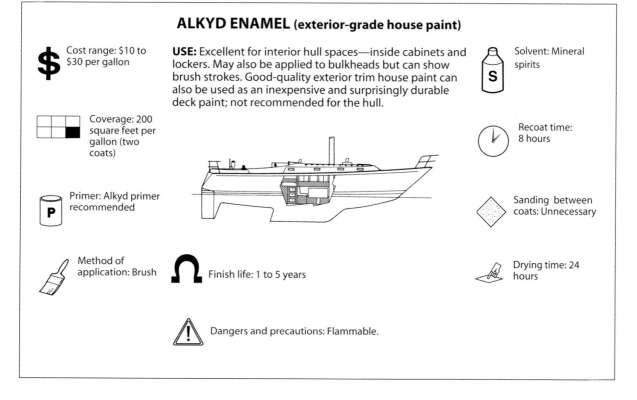

ALKYD ENAMEL (exterior-grade house paint)

$ Cost range: $10 to $30 per gallon

Coverage: 200 square feet per gallon (two coats)

P Primer: Alkyd primer recommended

Method of application: Brush

USE: Excellent for interior hull spaces—inside cabinets and lockers. May also be applied to bulkheads but can show brush strokes. Good-quality exterior trim house paint can also be used as an inexpensive and surprisingly durable deck paint; not recommended for the hull.

Finish life: 1 to 5 years

S Solvent: Mineral spirits

Recoat time: 8 hours

Sanding between coats: Unnecessary

Drying time: 24 hours

Dangers and precautions: Flammable.

TOPSIDE ENAMEL (marine alkyd enamel)

$ Cost range: $12 to $20 per quart.

USE: The least expensive hull and deck coating. Can be applied to almost any above-the-waterline surface. Compatible with most old coatings. Better hiding characteristics than polyurethane, but lower gloss and much shorter life. Good choice for interior surfaces.

S Recommended solvent: Proprietary or mineral spirits.

Coverage: 50 to 60 square feet per quart (two coats).

Recoat time: 24 hours.

P Primer required: Alkyd or epoxy undercoat required.

Sanding between coats: Recommended.

Method of application: Brush, roller, or spray.

Finish life: 2 to 3 years in exterior applications.

Drying time: 24 hours.

! Dangers and precautions: Flammable.

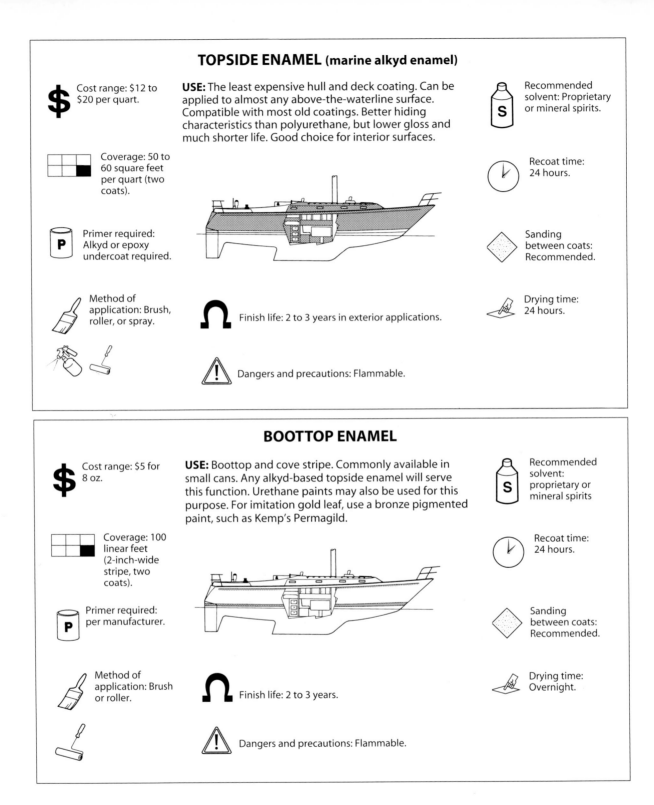

BOOTTOP ENAMEL

$ Cost range: $5 for 8 oz.

USE: Boottop and cove stripe. Commonly available in small cans. Any alkyd-based topside enamel will serve this function. Urethane paints may also be used for this purpose. For imitation gold leaf, use a bronze pigmented paint, such as Kemp's Permagild.

S Recommended solvent: proprietary or mineral spirits

Coverage: 100 linear feet (2-inch-wide stripe, two coats).

Recoat time: 24 hours.

P Primer required: per manufacturer.

Sanding between coats: Recommended.

Method of application: Brush or roller.

Finish life: 2 to 3 years.

Drying time: Overnight.

! Dangers and precautions: Flammable.

SINGLE-PART POLYURETHANE (urethane-modified alkyd)

$ Cost range: $15 to $20 per quart.

USE: Hull and deck finish. High gloss and good durability. Easier to apply than two-part paints. Fewer compatibility problems with old paint.

Recommended solvent: Proprietary or mineral spirits.

Coverage: 50 to 60 square feet per quart (two coats).

Recoat time: Overnight.

Primer required: Proprietary.

Sanding between coats: Recommended.

Method of application: Brush, roller, or spray.

Finish life: 3 to 5 years, with some loss of gloss.

Dangers and precautions: Flammable. Air-supplied respirator required for spray application.

Drying time: 24 hours.

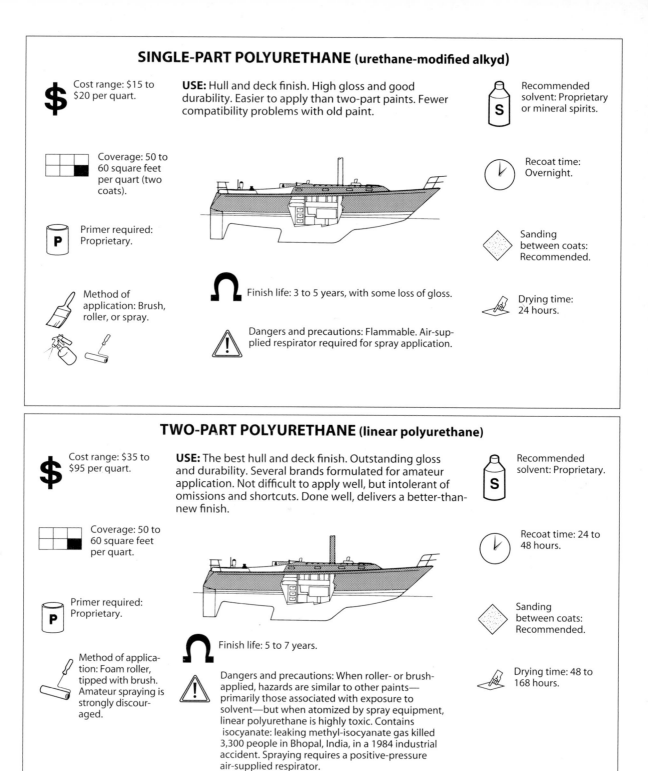

TWO-PART POLYURETHANE (linear polyurethane)

$ Cost range: $35 to $95 per quart.

USE: The best hull and deck finish. Outstanding gloss and durability. Several brands formulated for amateur application. Not difficult to apply well, but intolerant of omissions and shortcuts. Done well, delivers a better-than-new finish.

Recommended solvent: Proprietary.

Coverage: 50 to 60 square feet per quart.

Recoat time: 24 to 48 hours.

Primer required: Proprietary.

Sanding between coats: Recommended.

Method of application: Foam roller, tipped with brush. Amateur spraying is strongly discouraged.

Finish life: 5 to 7 years.

Dangers and precautions: When roller- or brush-applied, hazards are similar to other paints—primarily those associated with exposure to solvent—but when atomized by spray equipment, linear polyurethane is highly toxic. Contains isocyanate: leaking methyl-isocyanate gas killed 3,300 people in Bhopal, India, in a 1984 industrial accident. Spraying requires a positive-pressure air-supplied respirator.

Drying time: 48 to 168 hours.

LEMON OIL

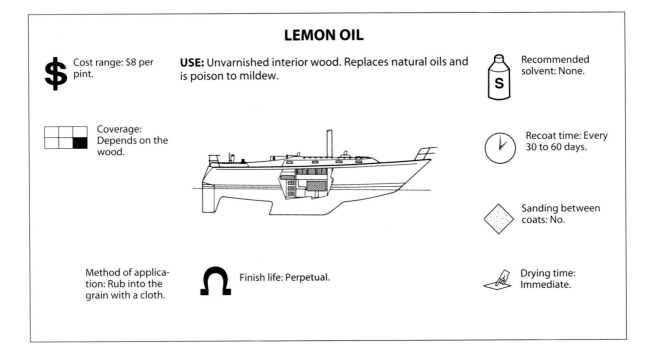

Cost range: $8 per pint.

Coverage: Depends on the wood.

Method of application: Rub into the grain with a cloth.

USE: Unvarnished interior wood. Replaces natural oils and is poison to mildew.

Finish life: Perpetual.

Recommended solvent: None.

Recoat time: Every 30 to 60 days.

Sanding between coats: No.

Drying time: Immediate.

LINSEED OIL

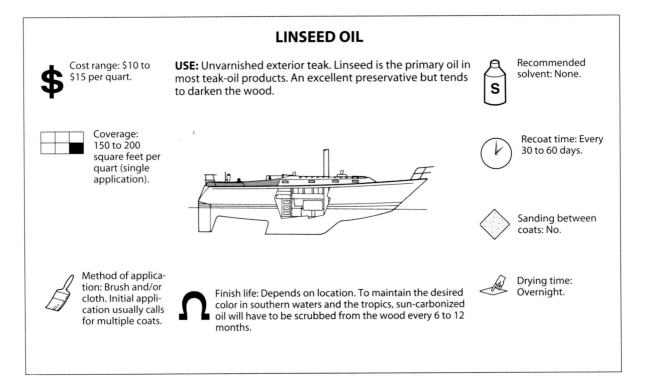

Cost range: $10 to $15 per quart.

Coverage: 150 to 200 square feet per quart (single application).

Method of application: Brush and/or cloth. Initial application usually calls for multiple coats.

USE: Unvarnished exterior teak. Linseed is the primary oil in most teak-oil products. An excellent preservative but tends to darken the wood.

Finish life: Depends on location. To maintain the desired color in southern waters and the tropics, sun-carbonized oil will have to be scrubbed from the wood every 6 to 12 months.

Recommended solvent: None.

Recoat time: Every 30 to 60 days.

Sanding between coats: No.

Drying time: Overnight.

TUNG OIL

$ Cost range: $12 to $17 per quart.

Coverage: 150 to 200 square feet per quart (single application).

USE: Unvarnished exterior teak. Tung oil is the base for some teak-oil products. More water-resistant than linseed oil and does not turn the wood dark. More expensive than linseed: if a teak product contains tung oil, it will be prominently mentioned on the label.

S Recommended solvent: None.

Recoat time: Every 30 to 60 days.

Sanding between coats: No.

Method of application: Brush and/or cloth. Initial application usually calls for multiple coats.

Finish life: Depends on location. To maintain the desired color in southern waters and the tropics, sun-carbonized oil will have to be scrubbed from the wood every 6 to 12 months.

Drying time: Overnight

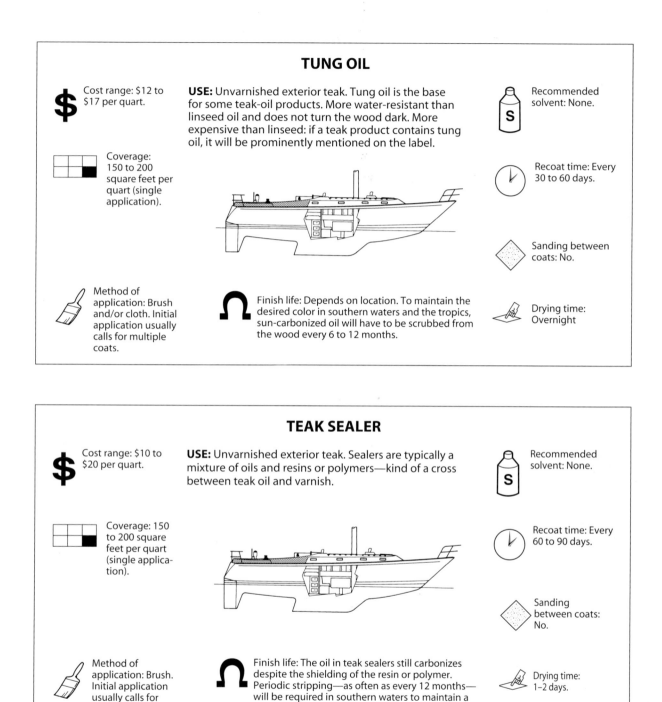

TEAK SEALER

$ Cost range: $10 to $20 per quart.

Coverage: 150 to 200 square feet per quart (single application).

USE: Unvarnished exterior teak. Sealers are typically a mixture of oils and resins or polymers—kind of a cross between teak oil and varnish.

S Recommended solvent: None.

Recoat time: Every 60 to 90 days.

Sanding between coats: No.

Method of application: Brush. Initial application usually calls for multiple coats.

Finish life: The oil in teak sealers still carbonizes despite the shielding of the resin or polymer. Periodic stripping—as often as every 12 months—will be required in southern waters to maintain a light color. Some formulations are pigmented to counteract darkening.

Drying time: 1–2 days.

SPAR VARNISH

$ Cost range: $10 to $30 per quart.

Coverage: 90 to 125 square feet per quart (one coat).

P Primer required: Thinned varnish.

Method of application: Brush. Minimum of five initial coats required, with the first two thinned as much as 50%.

USE: Clear finish for exterior and interior wood. Resin-based spar varnish is the least complicated wood finish and very long-lasting when properly maintained. Less abrasion-resistant than polyurethane but more flexible. Adds some color to the wood.

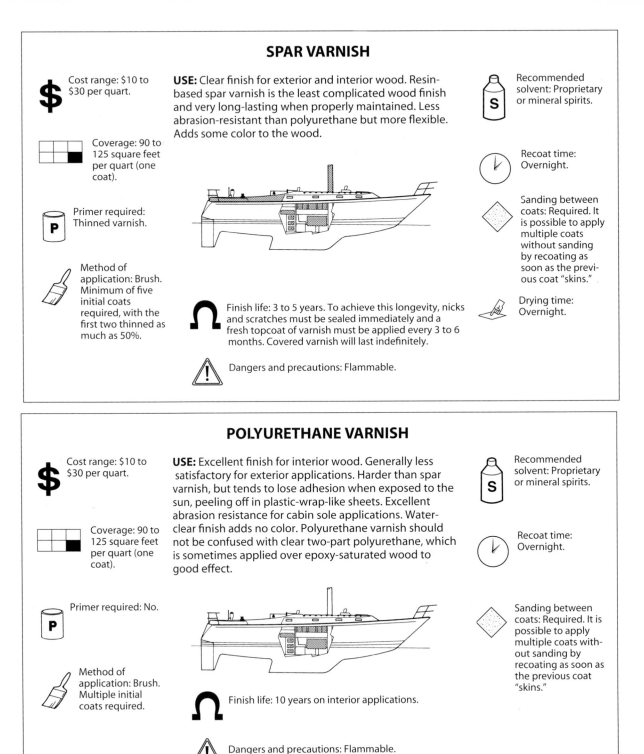

Finish life: 3 to 5 years. To achieve this longevity, nicks and scratches must be sealed immediately and a fresh topcoat of varnish must be applied every 3 to 6 months. Covered varnish will last indefinitely.

! Dangers and precautions: Flammable.

S Recommended solvent: Proprietary or mineral spirits.

Recoat time: Overnight.

Sanding between coats: Required. It is possible to apply multiple coats without sanding by recoating as soon as the previous coat "skins."

Drying time: Overnight.

POLYURETHANE VARNISH

$ Cost range: $10 to $30 per quart.

Coverage: 90 to 125 square feet per quart (one coat).

P Primer required: No.

Method of application: Brush. Multiple initial coats required.

USE: Excellent finish for interior wood. Generally less satisfactory for exterior applications. Harder than spar varnish, but tends to lose adhesion when exposed to the sun, peeling off in plastic-wrap-like sheets. Excellent abrasion resistance for cabin sole applications. Water-clear finish adds no color. Polyurethane varnish should not be confused with clear two-part polyurethane, which is sometimes applied over epoxy-saturated wood to good effect.

Finish life: 10 years on interior applications.

! Dangers and precautions: Flammable.

S Recommended solvent: Proprietary or mineral spirits.

Recoat time: Overnight.

Sanding between coats: Required. It is possible to apply multiple coats without sanding by recoating as soon as the previous coat "skins."

EPOXY

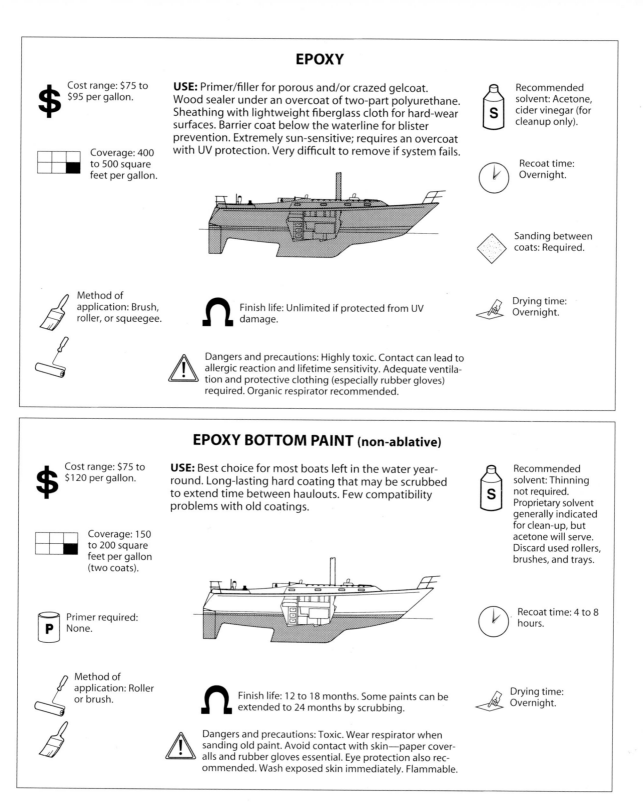

$ Cost range: $75 to $95 per gallon.

Coverage: 400 to 500 square feet per gallon.

USE: Primer/filler for porous and/or crazed gelcoat. Wood sealer under an overcoat of two-part polyurethane. Sheathing with lightweight fiberglass cloth for hard-wear surfaces. Barrier coat below the waterline for blister prevention. Extremely sun-sensitive; requires an overcoat with UV protection. Very difficult to remove if system fails.

S Recommended solvent: Acetone, cider vinegar (for cleanup only).

Recoat time: Overnight.

Sanding between coats: Required.

Method of application: Brush, roller, or squeegee.

Finish life: Unlimited if protected from UV damage.

Drying time: Overnight.

Dangers and precautions: Highly toxic. Contact can lead to allergic reaction and lifetime sensitivity. Adequate ventilation and protective clothing (especially rubber gloves) required. Organic respirator recommended.

EPOXY BOTTOM PAINT (non-ablative)

$ Cost range: $75 to $120 per gallon.

Coverage: 150 to 200 square feet per gallon (two coats).

P Primer required: None.

USE: Best choice for most boats left in the water year-round. Long-lasting hard coating that may be scrubbed to extend time between haulouts. Few compatibility problems with old coatings.

S Recommended solvent: Thinning not required. Proprietary solvent generally indicated for clean-up, but acetone will serve. Discard used rollers, brushes, and trays.

Recoat time: 4 to 8 hours.

Method of application: Roller or brush.

Finish life: 12 to 18 months. Some paints can be extended to 24 months by scrubbing.

Drying time: Overnight.

Dangers and precautions: Toxic. Wear respirator when sanding old paint. Avoid contact with skin—paper coveralls and rubber gloves essential. Eye protection also recommended. Wash exposed skin immediately. Flammable.

VINYL BOTTOM PAINT (non-ablative)

Cost range: $70 to $125 per gallon.

Coverage: 125-150 square feet per gallon (two coats).

Primer required: None.

Method of application: Roller or brush.

USE: Preferred by racers because surface is smoother than epoxy-based paint and can be burnished for lower friction. May be scrubbed to extend time between haulouts. Incompatible with most other paints; apply over vinyl paint or bare gelcoat only.

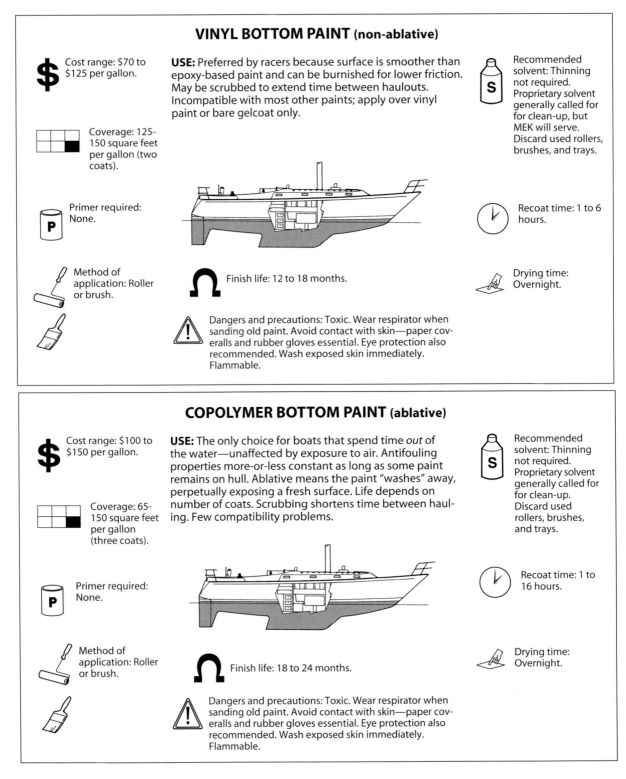

Finish life: 12 to 18 months.

Dangers and precautions: Toxic. Wear respirator when sanding old paint. Avoid contact with skin—paper coveralls and rubber gloves essential. Eye protection also recommended. Wash exposed skin immediately. Flammable.

Recommended solvent: Thinning not required. Proprietary solvent generally called for for clean-up, but MEK will serve. Discard used rollers, brushes, and trays.

Recoat time: 1 to 6 hours.

Drying time: Overnight.

COPOLYMER BOTTOM PAINT (ablative)

Cost range: $100 to $150 per gallon.

Coverage: 65-150 square feet per gallon (three coats).

Primer required: None.

Method of application: Roller or brush.

USE: The only choice for boats that spend time *out of* the water—unaffected by exposure to air. Antifouling properties more-or-less constant as long as some paint remains on hull. Ablative means the paint "washes" away, perpetually exposing a fresh surface. Life depends on number of coats. Scrubbing shortens time between hauling. Few compatibility problems.

Finish life: 18 to 24 months.

Dangers and precautions: Toxic. Wear respirator when sanding old paint. Avoid contact with skin—paper coveralls and rubber gloves essential. Eye protection also recommended. Wash exposed skin immediately. Flammable.

Recommended solvent: Thinning not required. Proprietary solvent generally called for for clean-up. Discard used rollers, brushes, and trays.

Recoat time: 1 to 16 hours.

Drying time: Overnight.

OTHER BOTTOM PAINTS

SOFT BOTTOM PAINT

Use: A good choice for slow-moving boats that get seasonal use. An ablative paint, but much softer and quicker to erode than copolymer. Inexpensive. Easy to sand and recoat. Scrubbing not recommended.
Cost range: $40 to $70 per gallon.
Coverage: 150 to 200 square feet per gallon (two coats).

THIN-FILM TEFLON

Use: Preferred by some racers for its low-friction surface. A thin, hard coating with some similarities to vinyl paint, but incorporating Teflon to reduce drag. Incompatible with some other paints. May be burnished.
Cost range: $100 to $130 per gallon.
Coverage: 100 square feet per gallon (three coats).

TIN-BASED PAINTS

Use: Generally banned in the United States except through special permit for aluminum hulls. Does not contribute to galvanic corrosion.
Cost range: $15 to $20 for 12 ounces.
Coverage: 1 square foot per ounce.

ZINC-OXIDE BASED PAINTS

Use: A relatively new formulation in the United States. Shows promise.

RACING ENAMEL

Use: No antifouling properties. Buffable slick finish for dry-stored racing boats.
Cost range: $50 to $70 per gallon.
Coverage: 400 square feet per gallon (two coats).

CUPROUS RESIN

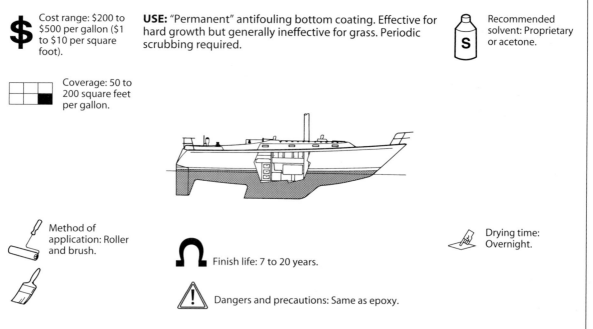

$ Cost range: $200 to $500 per gallon ($1 to $10 per square foot).

USE: "Permanent" antifouling bottom coating. Effective for hard growth but generally ineffective for grass. Periodic scrubbing required.

S Recommended solvent: Proprietary or acetone.

Coverage: 50 to 200 square feet per gallon.

Method of application: Roller and brush.

Finish life: 7 to 20 years.

Drying time: Overnight.

Dangers and precautions: Same as epoxy.

GELCOAT RESIN

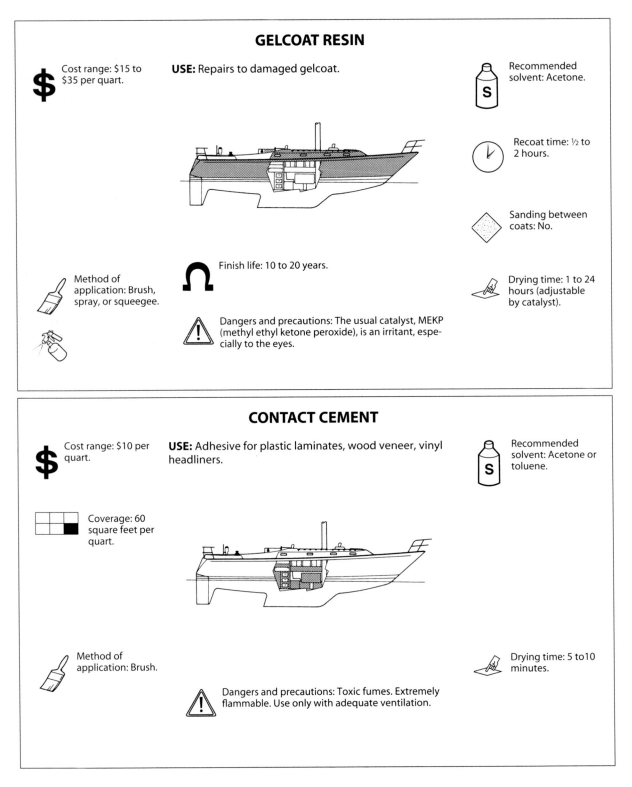

USE: Repairs to damaged gelcoat.

Cost range: $15 to $35 per quart.

Recommended solvent: Acetone.

Recoat time: ½ to 2 hours.

Sanding between coats: No.

Method of application: Brush, spray, or squeegee.

Finish life: 10 to 20 years.

Drying time: 1 to 24 hours (adjustable by catalyst).

Dangers and precautions: The usual catalyst, MEKP (methyl ethyl ketone peroxide), is an irritant, especially to the eyes.

CONTACT CEMENT

USE: Adhesive for plastic laminates, wood veneer, vinyl headliners.

Cost range: $10 per quart.

Recommended solvent: Acetone or toluene.

Coverage: 60 square feet per quart.

Method of application: Brush.

Drying time: 5 to10 minutes.

Dangers and precautions: Toxic fumes. Extremely flammable. Use only with adequate ventilation.

SILICONE SEALANT

$ Cost range: $6 to $10 per 10-ounce cartridge.

USE: Gaskets. Portlight bedding. Insulation between dissimilar metals. Not for use below the waterline.

Cleanup: Trim and "roll" off excess after cure.

Cure time: 1 to 7 days.

Method of application: Snug joint, then tighten after cure.

Seal life: 10 to 20 years.

POLYURETHANE SEALANT

$ Cost range: $7 to $15 per 10-ounce cartridge.

USE: A permanent sealant for through-hull fittings and hull-to-deck joints. High adhesive strength makes disassembly very difficult. May attack plastics—not recommended for portlights.

Cleanup: Mineral spirits or kerosene before cure.

Cure time: 2 to 7 days.

Method of application: Bead between parts to be assembled.

Seal life: 5 to 10 years.

POLYSULFIDE SEALANT

$ Cost range: $9 to $13 per 10-ounce cartridge.

USE: All-purpose sealant for bedding deck hardware, through-hull fittings, wood trim, etc. Caulking compound for teak decks. Good flexibility and allows for easier removal of bedded parts. May attack plastics—not recommended for portlights.

Cleanup: Trim and peel excess after cure.

Cure time: 2 to 7 days.

Method of application: Snug joint, then tighten after cure.

Seal life: 2 to 5 years.

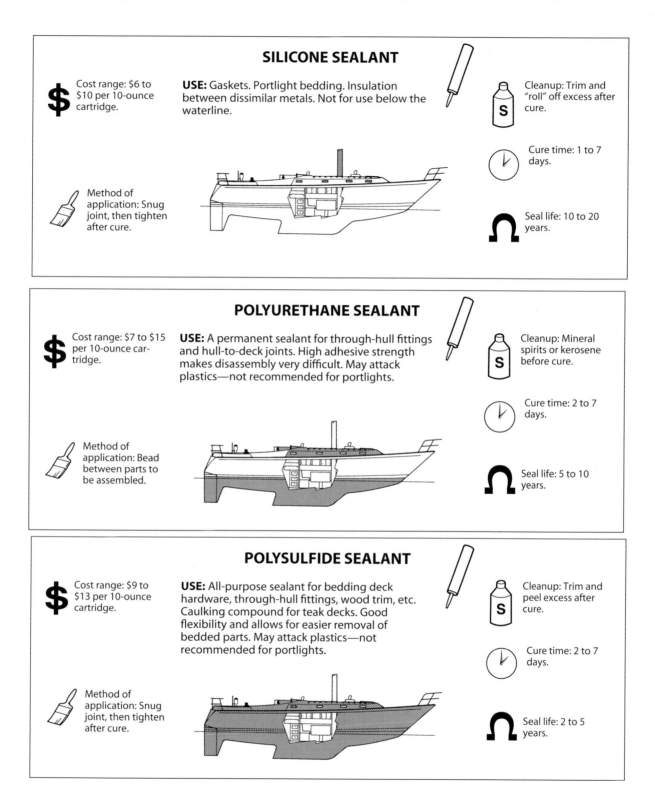

ACETONE

Cost range: $6 to $10 per gallon.

USE: Multipurpose solvent. Cleans epoxy, polyester, vinyl, lacquer, polyurethane paints and sealants, and contact cement and other adhesives.

Dangers and precautions: Avoid skin contact and excessive exposure to vapors. Extremely flammable.

MINERAL SPIRITS

Cost range: $4 to $5 per gallon.

USE: Multipurpose thinner and solvent. Can be used to thin most oil-based paints. Good brush cleaner.

Dangers and precautions: Avoid skin contact. Flammable.

MEK

Cost range: $8 to $12 per gallon.

USE: Similar uses to acetone, but takes ⅓ longer to evaporate.

Dangers and precautions: Same as acetone—avoid skin contact and excessive exposure to vapors. Flammable.

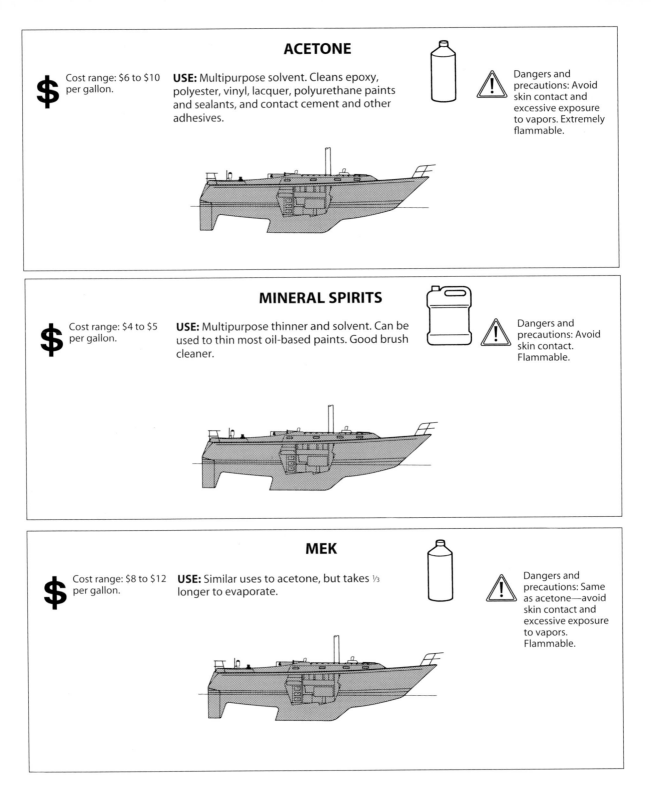

TOLUENE

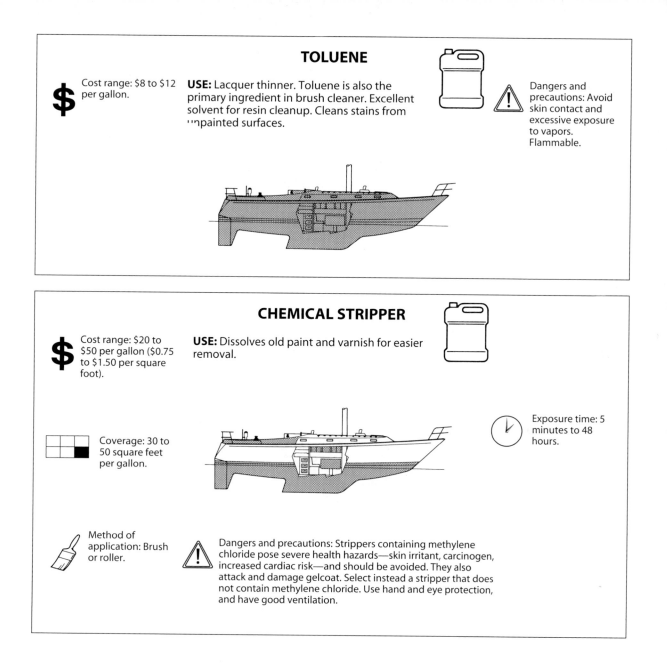

$ Cost range: $8 to $12 per gallon.

USE: Lacquer thinner. Toluene is also the primary ingredient in brush cleaner. Excellent solvent for resin cleanup. Cleans stains from unpainted surfaces.

Dangers and precautions: Avoid skin contact and excessive exposure to vapors. Flammable.

CHEMICAL STRIPPER

$ Cost range: $20 to $50 per gallon ($0.75 to $1.50 per square foot).

USE: Dissolves old paint and varnish for easier removal.

Coverage: 30 to 50 square feet per gallon.

Exposure time: 5 minutes to 48 hours.

Method of application: Brush or roller.

Dangers and precautions: Strippers containing methylene chloride pose severe health hazards—skin irritant, carcinogen, increased cardiac risk—and should be avoided. They also attack and damage gelcoat. Select instead a stripper that does not contain methylene chloride. Use hand and eye protection, and have good ventilation.

GOOD RESULTS FROM GOOD TOOLS

Good tools don't necessarily indicate craftsmanship, but craftsmanship always indicates quality tools. Whatever the refinishing job you are planning, do yourself a favor and select only the best-quality tools. Saving $10 on a second-rate brush may well cost you a second-rate finish—don't even consider it.

Not that throw-away brushes and 99-cent roller covers don't belong aboard your boat. *Au contraire*, many of the refinishing jobs aboard, especially prime coats or undercoats, are handled most effectively, economically, and ecologically (thinner is the villain) with toss-away brushes and rollers.

Even cheap brushes vary in quality, and cost is no indicator. Look for brushes dense with well-groomed bristles, then try to pull a few out. A brush that sheds like a St. Bernard in July is no good—period. Throw-away brushes that don't shed are a treasure; if you find some, buy a couple of dozen and hoard them (but paint with one before you invest).

JUDGING BRUSH QUALITY

To evaluate a brush, first examine the bristles. They should all be smooth and straight and flagged at the ends.

Press the bristles against the palm of your hand with a slight twisting motion. They should fan out evenly—not separate into clumps—then spring back into shape when you release them.

Part the bristles to see how they are set into the base. A plug is okay—the space it creates may enable the brush to carry more paint—but the plug should be no more than half the thickness of the base. Make sure the ferrule is solidly attached to the handle.

Remove any loose bristles—all new brushes have a few—by slapping the brush across the heel of your hand. Now give a few single bristles a tug. If any pull out, pick a different brush.

Finally, look for a brush that feels balanced and comfortable in your hand. A glossy coating on the handle will be easier to clean and have a better feel.

flagged bristle tip

plug

ferrule

heel

handle

THE RIGHT BRUSH FOR THE JOB

Paint-brush bristle is either natural or synthetic. Synthetic bristle—usually nylon or polyester—is favored by house painters because it is less affected by the water-based latex paints they use, but synthetic-bristle brushes have little to recommend them for most of the finishing jobs on a boat.

Most natural-bristle brushes are made from hog bristle, also called China (or Chinese) bristle because China is the largest hog-bristle supplier. Natural bristle is tapered, giving the tip of the brush a light touch that reduces the likelihood of leaving behind visible brush strokes in the finish. For fine finishwork, select a brush that is trimmed to a point or half-oval at the tip—called a "chisel" trim; this gives half the bristles the same "just touching" contact pressure on each stroke.

A good-quality China-bristle brush is adequate for all but the most demanding finishing jobs on a boat. For jobs requiring something better, an ox-hair brush, usually a blend of ox and hog bristle, is not a bad choice, but the best brushes are those made from bad-ger hair. A badger-hair brush is the brush of choice for tipping-out polyurethane or applying the last coat or two of varnish.

Brush width depends on the intended use. Select a 3-inch brush for tipping-out topside paint; a wider brush is more difficult to control and tends to contact the surface of the paint unevenly due to the curvature of the hull. For varnishing handrails and caprails, a 1½-inch brush is about right; accent trim may require a narrower brush, cabin sides and bulkheads a wider one. Your brush should never be wider than the surface you are painting.

Foam brushes have developed a dedicated following, especially for applying varnish, but most find that foam brushes don't deliver the same quality finish as a badger-hair brush. For small jobs the difference in the finish may be less significant than their convenience (no clean-up) and economy (1/20th the cost of badger hair), but don't start a large job with a foam brush without first comparing the results to a badger-hair brush for yourself. If you want to give foam a try, get a Jen polyfoam brush; they have distinctive, varnished handles, and the black foam heads are glued in place.

CLEANING TECHNIQUE

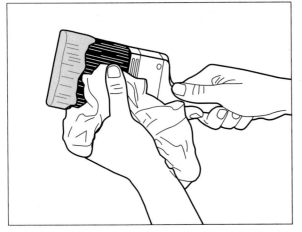

1 Pull the brush through a rag to remove any remaining paint.

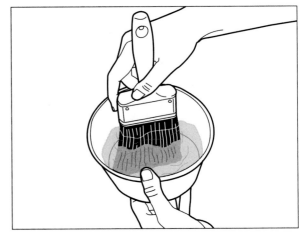

2 Press the brush into a small amount of thinner, twisting the brush slightly to spread the bristles.

3 Brush cleaning is much easier with a brush spinner—available for under $20 from most housepaint suppliers. Rinse and spin the brush several times, the final time in fresh thinner, to get it completely clean.

4 Comb the brush—any kind of comb will do—before you wrap the bristles.

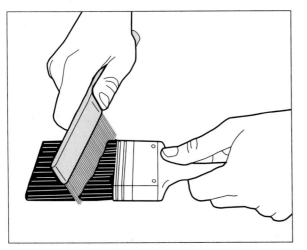

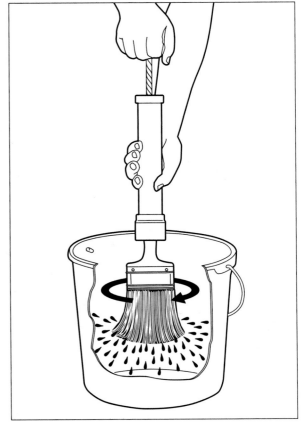

WRAPPING THE BRISTLES

A strip of paper grocery bag is ideal for wrapping a paintbrush. Pre-crease the paper down the middle, then place the tip of the brush just shy of the crease. A rubber band around the wrap at the ferrule will hold it in place and preserve the shape of the bristles. Throw-away brushes cleaned for reuse can be wrapped adequately in a folded paper towel.

ROLLER COVERS

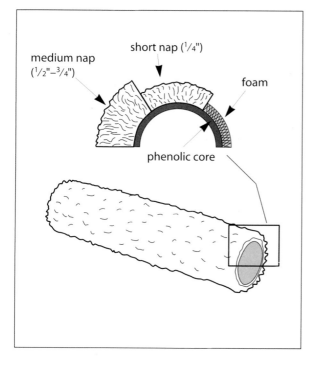

medium nap ($1/2$"–$3/4$")

short nap ($1/4$")

foam

phenolic core

Roller covers come in an array of quality, sizes, and nap lengths. For boat work, select only short nap (for antifouling bottom paint) or foam (for everything else). The one exception is molded-in nonskid, where a medium-nap roller may prove more effective. (A medium-nap roller might also be useful for coating roving-textured bilge and locker spaces, but brush application may be better.)

Cheap roller covers are adequate for bottom paint—you are not going to reuse them. Just be sure the nap is dense enough to hold paint and that it is firmly attached to the core.

For topside paint and other finishing uses, select the best foam rollers you can find. The aggressive solvents in polyurethane paints will dissolve standard foam roller covers; special covers with *phenolic cores* are required. To avoid unexpected disasters, make these the only kind of foam rollers aboard. Choose the 9-inch length for painting the hull; for the deck, 7-inch rollers may be handier.

CAGE-TYPE ROLLER HANDLE

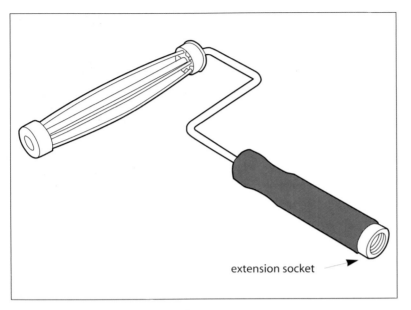

extension socket

Bird-cage-type frames make changing covers easier, and the frame gives the cover needed support in the middle. Three-inch frames are available for trim work.

CUTTING ROLLER COVERS FOR SPECIFIC NEEDS

For small areas such as boottops and narrow sections of the deck, shorter roller covers can be easier to control and do a better job. Cut standard 9-inch covers with a hacksaw to any required size. A 3-inch frame can be used with covers of various lengths.

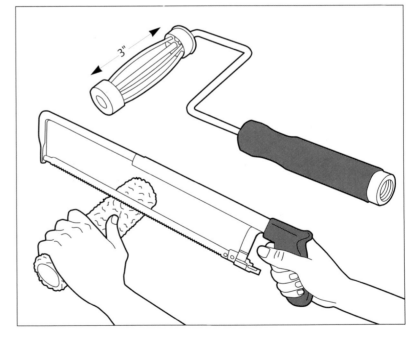

3"

SANDPAPER TYPES AND USES

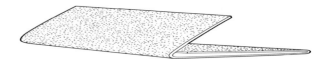

TYPE OF PAPER	IDENTIFYING COLOR	USES	SUGGESTED GRITS/COMMENTS	
Aluminum oxide	Tan or brown	Good all-around sandpaper	60D—rough sanding and paint removal; 120C—surface preparation for painting; 220A—between-coat sanding	The most useful paper; have plenty aboard
Emery cloth	Black	None	None	Except to prepare aluminum for paint, has no refinishing use; good for polishing metal and sharpening plane irons
Flint	Light beige or light gray	None	None	Dime-store sandpaper; useless—never buy flint paper
Garnet	Red	Hand sanding fine woodwork	None	Expensive and will not stand up to machine sanding; leave to the cabinetmakers
Silicon carbide (open coat)	White	Fine finishing paper; the best choice for sanding disks	180A—between-coat sanding; 400A—pre-polish sanding	Cuts well and relatively long-lasting; good choice for fine sanding
Silicon carbide (closed coat)	Black	Waterproof paper for wet sanding	340A—wet sanding between coats of polyurethane; 600A—pre-polish wet sanding	Called wet-or-dry sandpaper; wet sanding yields the finest finish

Grit numbers roughly represent the number of grains of grit per square inch—the higher the number the smaller the grains must be, so the higher the grit, the finer the finish.

The letter code following the grit designation—i.e., 60D or 400A—indicates the weight of the paper. A is the lightest and F is the heaviest (D is the heaviest commonly available for typical boat applications).

Sandpaper is available in four common grades—cabinet, production, premium, and industrial. Production paper—the grade most general suppliers carry—is adequate for all boat-refinishing jobs.

"Closed-coat" paper has the entire surface covered with abrasive; "open-coat" leaves the paper about 40% uncoated to reduce loading—clogging. Closed-coat is fine for wood and for hand sanding, but for reasonable paper life when power sanding, especially for sanding paints and varnish, select an open-coat paper.

Sandpaper is much cheaper if you buy it by the sleeve (50 or 100 sheets, depending on the grit) from a supply house. Per sheet price will be about half the individual sheet price at hardware stores.

DISK SANDER

A high-speed disk sander can make short work of paint removal. The disk sander has traditionally been used to quickly sand boat bottoms for their annual application of antifouling paint, but more stringent pollution requirements have already outlawed this method of bottom-paint removal in many parts of the country.

Do not try to substitute an electric drill with a polishing/sanding disk; a sander runs five times as fast and is designed for the continuous use and side loading associated with sanding. In the hands of a skillful operator, a disk sander is capable of extremely fine work in an amazingly short amount of time, but in less skilled hands it can just as quickly do a great deal of damage. A foam-padded disk allows the paper to adapt to a boat's curved surfaces and makes the sander more forgiving. If you can't find a padded disk sander, a glued-on pad will work fine. Using a disk sander well requires practice and concentration.

SANDING BLOCK

Almost all refinishing jobs require some hand sanding. To ensure a uniform surface, the sandpaper should be backed by some type of block, not the irregular tips of fingers. For flat surfaces a wooden block works well; for curved surfaces choose a rubber block or a flexible float. Attach the sandpaper to the blocks with disk adhesive.

ORBITAL SANDER

Unlike the disk sander, the orbital sander is almost risk free. No matter how inexperienced the operator, the only danger to the surface is perhaps sanding the finish off sharp edges. Despite its benign character, the orbital sander is the boat refinisher's greatest boon, saving hours on surface preparation.

Orbital sanders, also called finishing sanders, come in half-sheet and quarter-sheet models. A half-sheet sander may allow for the sanding of large areas a bit faster, but the quarter-sheet model (pictured), known as a *palm sander*, is more versatile and easier on the operator (you!). A finishing sander is an essential tool for all but the smallest refinishing projects. If you don't already own an orbital sander, buy one, and select a palm sander when you do.

FOLDING SANDPAPER FOR HAND SANDING

Some finger-backed sanding is likely. Fold the sandpaper as shown to keep the paper from sanding itself and to provide three fresh faces from each piece of paper. Wearing cloth garden gloves—the kind with the hard dots—will save the tips of your fingers.

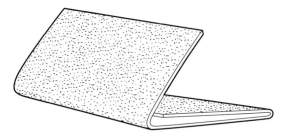

TIP: For heavy removal, such as bottom preparation, consider a random-bit sander. This useful tool combines the operations of both disk and orbital sanders.

SCRAPERS

When you repaint the bottom, scraping the old antifouling paint (with or without the application of a chemical paint remover) can be quicker than sanding and far easier on the lungs—yours and everybody else's.

For this particular task, use a 2½- or 3-inch hook scraper. If you aren't painting the bottom, leave hook scrapers at home with the latex paint and the synthetic-bristle brushes. The appropriate scrapers for all other boat refinishing are cabinet scrapers.

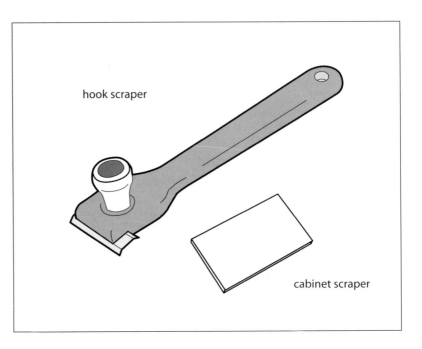

Learning to use a cabinet scraper effectively can save you a great deal of sanding (with expensive paper) and give you a much smoother surface. Scrapers are especially effective on wood surfaces prior to varnishing.

Hold the cabinet scraper tilted slightly toward you—at about 75° with the surface—and draw the scraper toward you. The blade should produce very fine shavings; if not, it needs to be sharpened.

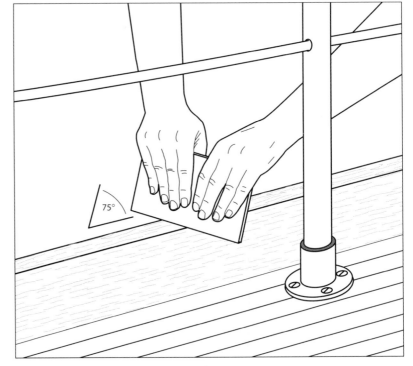

SHARPENING A SCRAPER

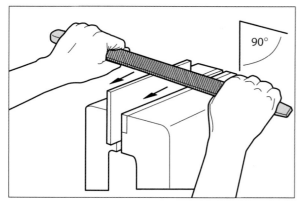

1 Draw a mill file across the edge to square it.

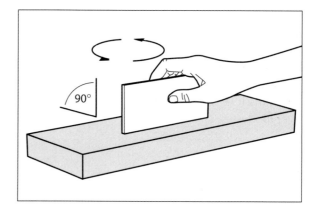

2 Whet each edge on an oil stone. If you are sharpening a hook-scraper blade, stop right here; never burnish the blade of a hook scraper.

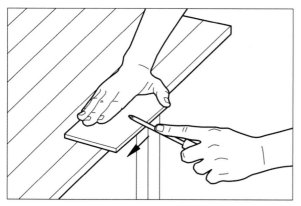

3 Burnish the sides of a cabinet scraper flat with a burnishing tool or the round shank of a Phillips screwdriver.

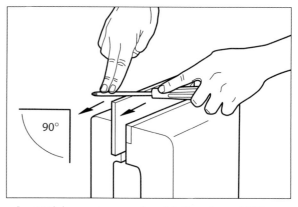

4 With heavy pressure, burnish the edges at 90°.

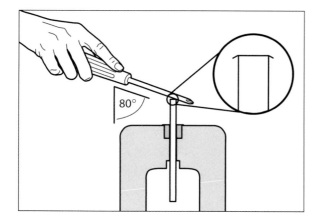

5 Tilt the shank about 10° and burnish one corner of the edge to 80°. Tilt the shank the other way and burnish the opposite edge. When you have burnished the entire perimeter, you will have eight fresh cutting edges.

RAGS

For any finishing project, you can never have too many rags. The best rags are cotton diapers—very absorbent and completely dye free. Marine suppliers and boatyard stores sell them by the pound.

DISPOSABLE COVERALLS AND CAP

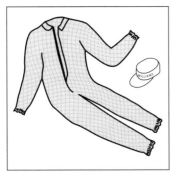

Old clothes are the usual painting uniform, but for less than $10 you can buy a paper-like coverall that will provide better dust (and fiberglass) protection. A painter's cap will protect your hair and/or scalp.

GLOVES, GOGGLES, AND RESPIRATOR

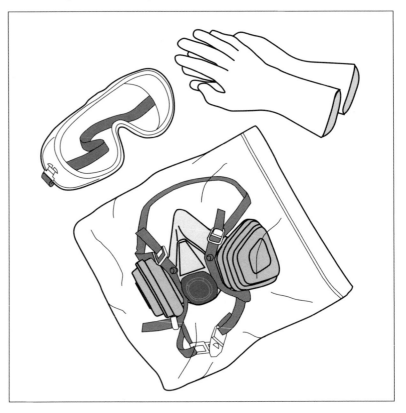

Some paints, especially bottom paints and two-part polyurethanes, require a higher degree of protection than mere coveralls. Avoid skin, eye, and lung exposure to their chemical components or their fumes. Be sure the gloves you buy are unaffected by the solvents you will be using.

A paper dust mask is inadequate protection from toxic bottom-paint dust—buy a comfortable respirator. None of the coatings you will be using are especially dangerous (assuming you are not spraying polyurethane), but as long as you have a respirator, use it—you'll need those lungs when you're 80. Replace the cartridges in your respirator if they aren't fresh, and replace them again as soon as you smell fumes (organic cartridges) or breathing requires any noticeable effort (dust/mist filters). Keep your organic respirator in a sealed plastic bag when you aren't using it.

PREPARATION

Genius is one percent inspiration and ninety-nine percent perspiration.
—Thomas Alva Edison

Brilliance is one percent application and ninety-nine percent preparation. Most people seem to think that a coat or two of paint will cover—meaning hide— all but the most serious surface flaws. Perhaps the source of this fiction is experience with interior wall paints—thick, rubbery coatings that dry to a flat (nonreflective) finish. Closer inspection will reveal that even these don't hide gouges and depressions, they merely camouflage them with uniform color.

It is not just color but gloss that we prize in a boat finish. The paints and varnishes used on a boat, with the exception of bottom paint, are formulated to provide that gem-like brilliance. Such high-gloss finishes accentuate every underlying surface flaw.

The bad news, then, is that your finish can never be better than the surface it is applied to; but there is good news. Because the gelcoat was originally sprayed into a highly polished mold, surface flaws on fiberglass boats are usually limited and easy to correct. As for brightwork, sanding the wood to a perfectly smooth surface—all that is required for that perfect varnish coating— is not difficult, but because the varnish is essentially clear, the wood must also have a uniform color. This second part presents more of a challenge.

When you prepare the surface, a lick and a promise will not be good enough. It will have to be mirror-smooth before you coat it if you want it to be mirror-smooth afterward. Every extra little bit you put into surface preparation will pay dividends in how the final finish looks, so don't cut corners. But don't get crazy either: it's a boat, not a Steinway.

REMOVING TRIM AND HARDWARE

Removing as much hardware and trim as practical from the surface to be painted makes painting much easier—you can roll right over the spot where the bow cleats are mounted rather than carefully painting around them with a brush. The quality of the finish will also be enhanced since it is much harder to get a stroke-free finish from paint applied with a brush than from rolled-on paint lightly tipped with a brush.

Removing hardware and trim also eliminates many "edges" where the paint stops. Paint failure usually begins at these edges, so having the paint skin extend under bedded hardware is best.

Bungs—wooden plugs—in a piece of trim mean it is screwed in place. If the bungs were set dry or with varnish, you can remove them by drilling a small-diameter hole in the center and running a screw through it; when the point stops against the underlying screw head, continuing to turn the screw lifts the bung. Unfortunately this can also lift the wood around the hole. A safer method is to use a bit just slightly smaller than the bung to drill out most of it, then collapse the remaining ring of plug with a small chisel.

Deck-mounted handrails are often bolted in place from inside the cabin. Sometimes the bolts are hidden by trim, matching interior handrails, or a removable head-liner. If the handrails are mounted with screws, replace them with bolts when you reinstall the handrails.

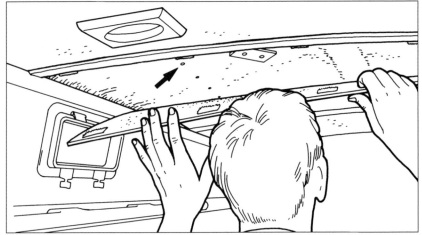

While painting the deck is a good time to replace crazed portlights and to service and re-bed opening portholes. Frames are usually through-bolted, but if the mounting screws thread into the frame, expect some difficulty in removing them without damaging the threaded socket. Drilling and through-bolting may be necessary to re-install the frame (see *Sailboat Hull and Deck Repair* in this series for more information).

TIP: Interior wood trim is often attached to plywood or formica with finishing nails. Inspection may reveal where the holes are patched. To release the trim drive the nails all the way through it with a nail set. Glued trim can be lifted with a sharpened drywall knife driven under the trim. Lift both sides of a corner molding before trying to remove the piece.

Cleats and stanchion bases should be through-bolted. Make sure the screw-driver is the correct size for the slot. To run less risk of damaging the slot, release the fastener by loosening the nut under-neath, not by turning the bolt with the screwdriver. An open-end wrench on the square shank of the screwdriver can make holding it against the torque of the wrench on the nut easier.

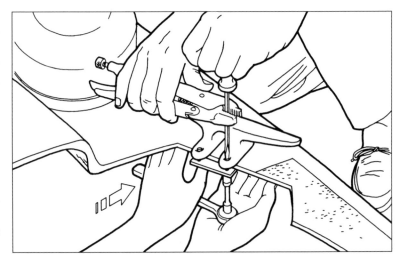

CLEANING

Preparation always begins with cleaning the surface. Use liquid laundry detergent (like Wisk) for most of your cleaning jobs. For better results, boost your detergent solution with trisodium phosphate (TSP), available in any hardware store. If the surface has any mildew, add a cup of chlorine bleach (Clorox) per gallon of water to the mix, and let the surface stand wet for about 30 minutes, then wash it again without the bleach. Be sure you rinse the surface completely free of all detergent residue.

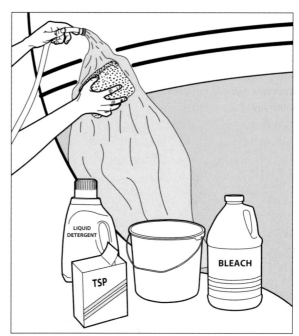

DEGREASING

Oil or grease on the surface will ruin the finish, and soap solutions may fail to remove these. Use a rag soaked with MEK to degrease the surface. (Acetone can also be used, but MEK evaporates more slowly to hold the contaminants in suspension longer. For wiping bare wood, the quick-flashing acetone will be less likely to raise the grain.)

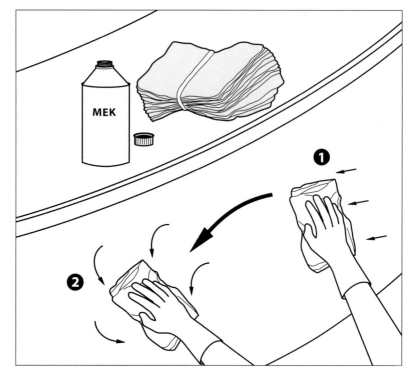

Wet the surface thoroughly with the solvent-soaked rag, then "sweep" the rag in one direction—like sweeping crumbs from a counter—to pick up the suspended contaminants. Turn the folded rag often, taking care not to reuse any areas. Change the rag when all areas have been used.

REMOVING ANY TRACE OF SILICONE

Silicone on the surface is just as ruinous as grease, and almost all boat waxes and polishes for the last 20 years have contained silicone. Even if the surface has never been waxed, the mold was, and the gelcoat almost certainly still retains traces of the mold release wax. Always dewax the surface *before* any sanding; otherwise the sandpaper drags the silicone into the scratches and it becomes very difficult to remove.

Silicone is resistant to detergents and many solvents—that's what makes it such a popular wax additive. *All* bare fiberglass, and all painted surfaces if there is any possibility that they may have been waxed, must be wiped down with a silicone-removing solvent—called wash, prep, or dewaxer by various manufacturers.

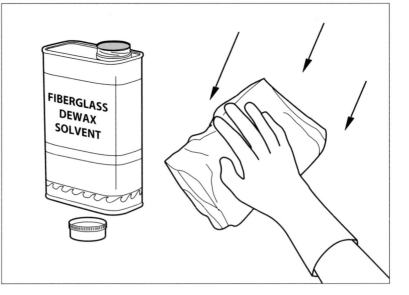

Soak a folded cloth with the wax remover and wipe it slowly across the surface in a single direction, again in a sweeping pattern. Change the contact surface of the cloth regularly.

CHECKING THE OLD PAINT WITH SOLVENT

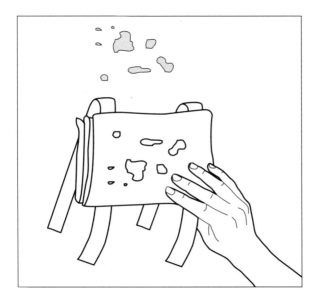

Check previously painted surfaces for compatibility by applying a rag soaked with the solvent for the new paint to the surface and leaving it for 10 minutes. If it lifts the surface, the old paint will have to be removed or sealed with a conversion coat—a paint or primer with a less aggressive solvent system. Perform this test in an inconspicuous spot.

CHECKING THE OLD PAINT WITH TAPE

No matter how tenaciously your new paint adheres to the old, if the old paint has lost its grip, early failure is guaranteed. If your old paint fails this test, it all has to come off. On the bright side, it may not be all that hard to remove.

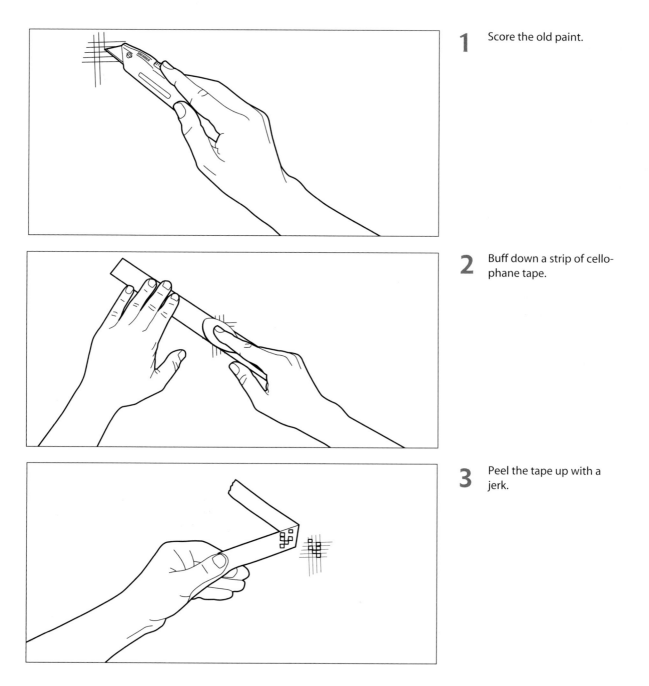

1 Score the old paint.

2 Buff down a strip of cellophane tape.

3 Peel the tape up with a jerk.

USING CHEMICAL STRIPPER

Gelcoat and paint are chemically similar, so many paint strippers also attack gelcoat. Select a stripper specifically labeled for use on fiberglass, and do not leave it on the surface longer than recommended.

Most strippers contain methylene chloride—read the label. Methylene chloride is extremely hazardous—a known carcinogen with a rogues' gallery of other serious effects on the heart, lungs, liver, and nervous system. Protect yourself with gloves, goggles, and an organic respirator.

1 Coat only as much surface area as you can scrape in five minutes.

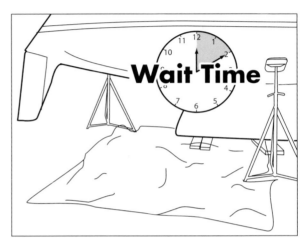

2 Wait the specified time—usually 5 to 10 minutes.

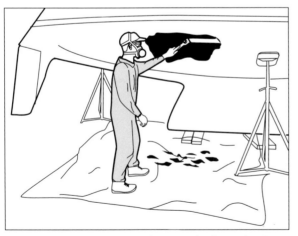

3 Remove lifted paint with a putty knife or a hook scraper.

4 Rinse away residue with water or the recommended proprietary wash.

POWER SANDING WITH A DISK SANDER

No sanding tool removes material faster than the disk sander. A disk with a foam pad will make the sander much more effective for the rounded surfaces of boats. For bottom-paint removal, select 80-grit open-coat aluminum-oxide sanding disks. For finer work, use 180- or 220-grit open-coat paper. The disk sander is not recommended for stripping old varnish because of the risk to the wood.

Always tilt the disk slightly so that only one side is in contact with the surface. Use only light pressure; the disk sander gets its effectiveness from speed, not force. Moving the sander rapidly across the surface is generally the best technique, i.e., several quick passes rather than a single slow one. Care and concentration are required to prevent damage to the surface. Letting the spinning disk linger too long in one spot also heats the finish, making it soften and tend to load the paper.

A random-orbit sander can be a good compromise—slower, but safer. Hold the disk of a random-orbit sander flat against the surface.

"SAFE" STRIPPER—A BETTER ALTERNATIVE

A NEW TYPE OF CHEMICAL STRIPPER—the so-called "safe stripper"—is a less hazardous alternative. Safe strippers contain no methylene chloride. They are not Evian, of course—they still contain toxic chemicals—but the health hazard for these products is typically classified as only moderate compared to severe for any product containing methylene chloride.

The most effective safe strippers rely on N-methyl-2-pyrolidone. This type of stripper is actually more effective at removing paint than methylene chloride and has no effect on gelcoat. The only drawback to these strippers is that they take much longer to do the job. They must be left on the surface as long as 48 hours. Cost range for these products is $.50 to $1.00 per square foot.

USING A PALM SANDER

No precautions are required to use an orbital palm sander. Material removal is deliberate and smooth. This is the best tool for preparing a surface for paint or varnish, and it makes short work of between-coat sanding.

As a general rule, preparing a surface for an initial coat of paint or varnish calls for 120-grit paper. The scratches left by this grit are fine enough not to show through the finish while still providing adequate "tooth" for the paint or varnish. For wood in poor condition, start with 60-grit, then 80-grit, and finally 120-grit. This will be smooth enough for teak or mahogany, but harder woods like walnut and oak may benefit from an additional sanding pass with 180- or even 220-grit.

You can make the job go faster if you load the sander with three or four sheets of paper at a time. When the surface layer stops creating dust, slice it away with a knife to reveal fresh paper.

Use 180- or 220-grit paper for between-coat sanding of both varnish and paint. The exception to this is two-part polyurethane, which needs to be wet sanded with 340-grit wet-or-dry paper between coats. NEVER WET SAND WITH AN ELECTRIC SANDER. However, the same effect can be achieved by misting the surface with a spritzer bottle and running the sander over the misted area. But keep in mind that water and electricity are a deadly combination, so take care to keep the sander dry. Rubber gloves are recommended as a precaution.

The high speeds of palm sanders—about 14,000 rpm—can result in an ear-damaging shriek. Ear plugs are available from any drugstore for about a buck; buy a pair and use them. Not only will they save your hearing, but by eliminating the fatigue that accompanies such an assault on the senses, they actually make the job much easier.

HAND SANDING

1 Machine sanding is not always possible: access may be restricted, the shape of the surface may be irregular, or the job may simply be a small one. When hand sanding wood in preparation for any kind of coating, always sand with the grain; cross-grain sanding will leave visible scratches.

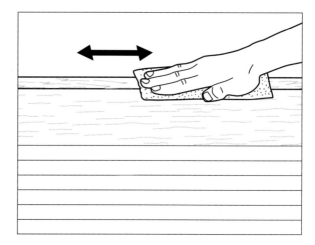

2 Sanding slightly across the grain with a float can be effective for fairing wood with ridges or "wows" (depressions). Starting with 80-grit paper, limit the angle off the grain line to no more than 30°. Sand diagonally across the grain from both directions before finishing with the grain, using 100- and 120-grit paper.

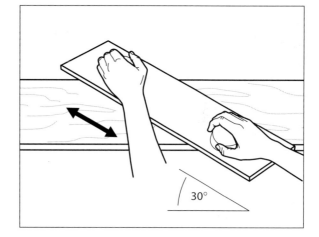

3 For hand sanding gelcoat and painted surfaces, direction is not important. The main concerns are to avoid introducing wows into the surface—a rubber sanding block is usually a good idea—and to select a grit fine enough not to leave scratches that will show through the coating. Use 120-grit paper if you are applying an undercoat, 220 if the coat will be the top one.

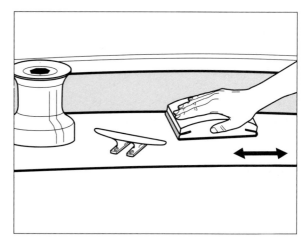

CLEANING RAW WOOD AFTER SANDING

1 The most effective way to remove dust from raw wood is with a vacuum cleaner and a brush attachment.

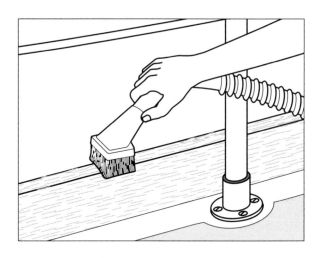

2 If that is unavailable, use a vigorous motion with a dense (and clean) paintbrush or shopbrush to sweep the dust out of the grain.

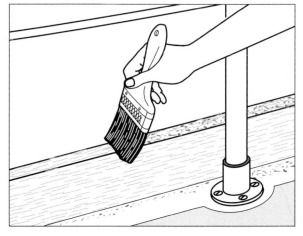

3 Finally, wipe the wood in a single direction with a cloth soaked with the thinner for the coating you are about to apply; using a commercial tack cloth can introduce substances incompatible with some coatings.

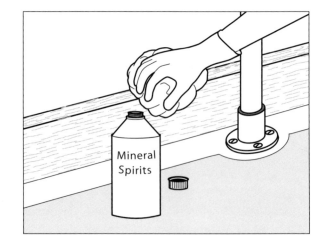

CLEANING FINISHED SURFACES

Flushing with water is the best way to remove dust from painted and varnished surfaces. Use a clean cloth to scrub the surface while flooding with a hose. When the surface is completely dry—watch out for water collecting in cracks, crevices, and joints—wipe it a final time with a solvent-soaked cloth before applying the coating.

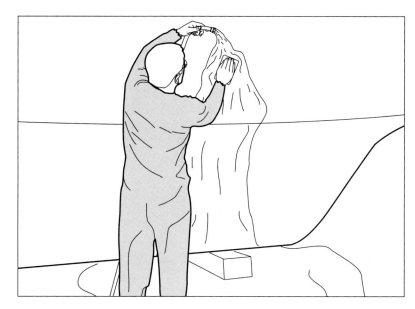

WETTING DOWN AROUND THE PAINT AREA

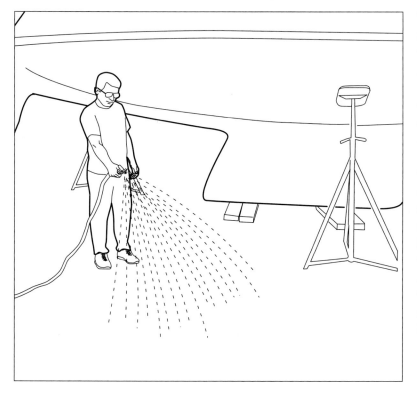

To keep the dust down, it is almost always a good idea to wet down the immediate area before varnishing or painting. Below decks, misting cushions, counters, and cabin soles with a fine spray from a spritzer can help give fresh varnish a chance to skin dust-free.

One caution: when applying two-part polyurethane, be careful about wetting the area on a hot, still day. The water may "steam," raising the humidity around the boat, and causing you problems with this moisture-sensitive paint. Any breeze—the reason you need to wet the ground anyway—should prevent any localized increase in humidity.

INSIDE THE CABIN

If you have limited experience applying paint or varnish, start your project in the interior of your boat. You will find plenty of surfaces that will benefit from a fresh coat of paint no matter how lubberly the application. For example, the area beneath bunk and settee cushions, often dirty, water-stained, or mildewed, presents a convenient surface to work on your roller and brush techniques. The fresh paint will protect the wood regardless of how it is applied, and any mistakes you make will be hidden by the cushions.

The interior of lockers and cabinets also provide risk-free surfaces for getting comfortable with the process and tools of refinishing. Brighten raw fiberglass lockers with a coat of paint. White is a good choice, but selecting a pastel can add an unexpected bit of cheer. To make the most of this effect, paint the inside of the doors and the underside of the access hatches.

Choose *alkyd* enamel for interior refinishing. Select low-luster exterior trim house paint; it is tough, washable, less expensive than marine paints, and available in an infinite selection of colors. It is perfect for lockers, bilges, and under-cushion furniture. Many boatowners like it for bulkheads as well.

For bulkheads covered with a plastic laminate, a roller-applied coating of single-part polyurethane—there is little need for the extra durability of two-part paint—can yield a surface that is indistinguishable in appearance from new laminate. Adding a little flattener generally produces a more pleasing effect.

Wood trim below decks may be maintained oiled or varnished with equal success. For oiling, choose *lemon oil* (not lemon polish or lemon wax). It won't stand up to the rigors of exterior exposure—you need linseed oil or tung oil for that—but lemon oil is wonderful below. It feeds the wood, replacing natural oils, it is poison to mildew, and it smells good.

If you plan to varnish the interior wood, choose polyurethane varnish often called urethane). Urethane varnish generally doesn't do well on exterior wood, but for interior use it is superior to spar varnish. It provides a harder, more durable surface; protected from the sun it can last indefinitely. Polyurethane's toughness makes it the best choice for a varnished sole, and the polyurethane is not as slick as oil-based varnish when it gets wet.

Remove trim or protect it with tape. Check compatibility of old paint with a thinner-soaked rag. Scrub the surface and bleach if mildew is present. (Adding bleach to the cleaning solution is almost always a good idea on a boat.) Set hatches, drawers, and doors aside to paint separately. Sand with 120-grit paper and wipe the surface dust-free with mineral spirits (if you are painting with alkyd enamel).

POURING PAINT AND RESEALING THE CONTAINER

1   Opening a paint or varnish can with a screwdriver will distort it and can prevent it from resealing; always use a paint-can opener. If you stir varnish at all, do it slowly and carefully to avoid introducing bubbles. Paint, on the other hand, can be stirred vigorously and must be stirred until there is no difference between the paint pulled up by the bottom of your stirrer and that at the top.

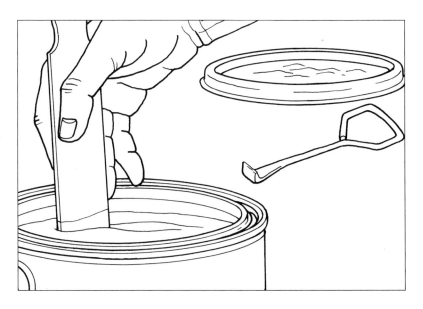

2 Never paint out of the can the paint comes in; that causes the paint to thicken from extended air exposure, and you introduce contaminants—loose bristles, dried paint, dust, and insects—to all your paint. Pour up as much as you will use in an hour or so into a convenient-size container—a clean discard from the kitchen or galley will do, or for a few cents buy one of the plastic paint buckets commercially available.

3 Close the container as soon as you have poured your paint. To make sure the can seals properly and that you can get it open next time, always clean the paint out of the can rim before replacing the lid. A ½-inch throw-away brush makes short work of this essential task, and it can be kept soft in a little thinner until the job is done. Press the lid closed with your thumbs—**do not hammer it closed** unless you are using a rubber mallet.

may compromise lid seal

USING A PAINT FILTER

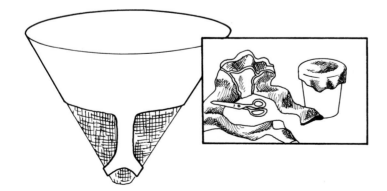

Even sealed paint can "skin," and broken bits of this semi-dried paint will ruin your finish. Filter all paint and varnish before you use it. Cone-shaped mesh filters can be purchased for 15 or 20 cents, or you can accomplish the same thing for free by stretching a section of discarded pantyhose over your bucket before pouring the paint into it.

THINNING

Thinning is the secret. If your paint is thinned perfectly, any numskull can get a great finish. A little off, and you can compensate some with good brush and roller technique. Get too wide of the mark and you may be driven to cut off an ear.

It needn't come to that. Proper thinning just requires patience.

If the brush or roller drags, the paint needs thinning. Too little thinner will prevent the paint from leveling, showing every brush stroke. Add too much thinner and the paint sags and runs, and much of the gloss will be lost. The trick is to sneak up on the perfect viscosity by adding a little thinner at a time and testing the results. Thin only the paint you are using, never your supply.

Thinner evaporates quickly, so the flow characteristics of your paint can change as you use it, particularly on a hot day. If that begins to happen, stir a few drops of thinner into your batch periodically, but remember that the less paint you have left, the less thinner it will take to achieve the desired effect. Go s-l-o-w-l-y.

With fresh paint, never add more than a capful of thinner at a time. You will spill far less thinner if you pour it with the spout up. Stir the thinner in thoroughly, then try the new mix on a test surface—a piece of glass is ideal. Keep adding a capful, mixing, and testing until the paint flows out the way you want. If it starts to sag or run (your test surface must be vertical), you have added too much thinner. Correct this by adding paint, but keep in mind that it will take a cupful of paint to offset the effects of a capful of thinner.

BRUSHING TECHNIQUES

1 Dip the *tip* of the brush into the paint—never deeper than ⅓ the bristle length.

2 Unload one side by dragging the brush over an edge.

For small jobs, the side of the bucket will serve; for larger painting projects, a piece of stiff wire (coat-hanger wire is perfect) installed across the bucket through a pair of punched holes will prevent the paint from finding its way to the outside of the bucket. A straight wire also introduces fewer bubbles into varnish.

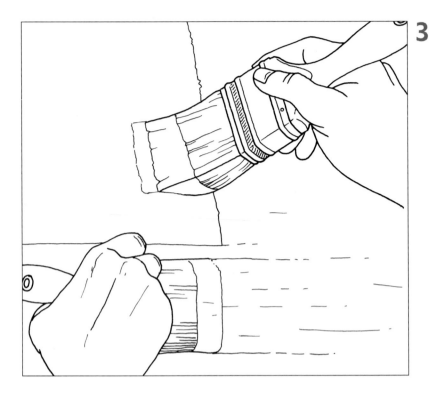

3 Apply the paint—loaded side first—just beyond the wet edge. Use several straight back-and-forth strokes to join the paint to the previously painted area and to spread it evenly. You can brush enamel as much as you like, but when applying varnish, limit your strokes to the absolute minimum required. A good varnisher will try to use only three or four—one to apply, one or two to spread, and one to finish.

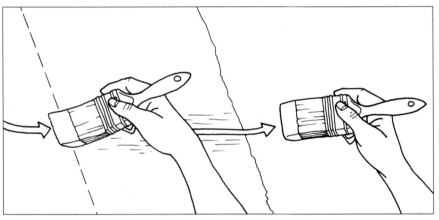

4 Finish by blending the new paint into the previous brush load. The usual method is to brush into the previously painted area, lifting the brush while the stroke is still in motion, but the best finish is achieved if the final stroke is outward. Start this stroke 6 inches behind the old wet edge, but don't let the bristles actually touch the paint until a couple of inches behind it. Think of landing an airplane—very softly. Continue this light stroke to the new wet edge. The advantage of this outward stroke is it pushes excess paint forward rather than back onto the previous application.

USING A PAINT ROLLER

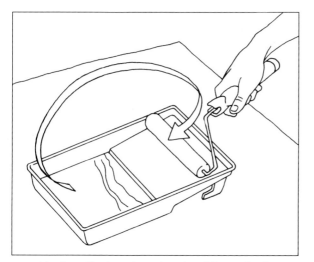

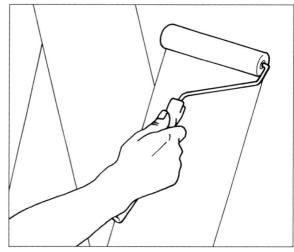

1 Dip the roller into the paint, then lift it and roll it **down** the slope to even the load and unload any excess paint. To avoid end tracks, unload the ends by tilting the roller and rolling each end down the slope with heavy pressure.

2 Apply the paint initially with a W or M motion, then continue to roll the surface until the coverage is complete and uniform. The direction of your strokes is not important—whatever is most convenient.

TIPPING FOR A SMOOTHER FINISH

Rolling leaves most paints with a slight orange-peel-like texture. This texture, similar to that found on many plastic laminates, can give an attractive, light-diffusing surface particularly suitable for bulkheads. For a smoother finish, such as a hull application, tip the rolled-on paint immediately with a first-quality brush. Tipping involves no more than dragging the tip of a dry brush—meaning not dipped in paint—over the surface immediately after the paint has been rolled on.

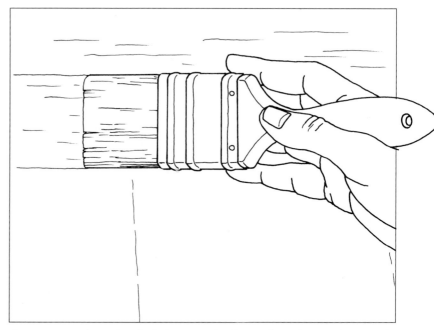

One or two strokes using the lightest touch will turn the surface to glass. Touch and lift with the stroke in motion to keep from introducing stroke marks.

KEEPING TOOLS AND PAINT FRESH

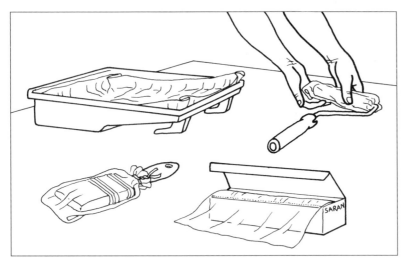

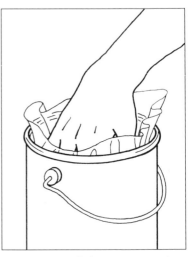

1 When you need a break, wrap your roller cover or brush in kitchen wrap—don't bind the nap or bristles tightly, just seal out the air. Keep the paint in your tray or bucket fresh by pressing a piece of plastic wrap onto the surface.

2 A piece of plastic wrap on the surface of leftover paint and pressed against the sides of the can will insulate the paint from air in the can and greatly extend its shelf life. Peel the plastic from the surface, and filter the paint to use it.

PREPARING PLASTIC LAMINATE FOR PAINTING

A HUGE NUMBER OF BOATS have been delivered with bulkheads covered with plastic laminate. Too often that laminate has been in a woodgrain pattern. Too much wood already tends to make boat cabins cave-dark anyway, and then for it to lack the warmth, texture, and smell of real wood is barely tolerable. If this sounds like elitist drivel to you, for your next wedding anniversary try giving a bouquet of plastic long-stem roses. You will quickly change your view on the importance of aesthetics.

The one good characteristic of woodgrain plastic laminate—of all plastic laminate, for that matter—is that it makes an excellent substratum for paint. The surface of plastic laminate is melamine resin (over a photograph of real wood, in case you wondered). Melamine resin is a tough, heat-resistant plastic. It is also slippery—the quality that gives it its legendary stain-resistance.

For paint to get a good grip on melamine, that slippery surface has to be roughened. Load your palm sander with 80-grit paper and thoroughly sand all the laminate to be painted to a uniform dullness, changing to fresh paper whenever the sander quits generating white plastic dust. Switch to 120-grit paper and sand the entire surface again to provide a final surface with adequate tooth, but with scratches fine enough to be completely hidden by the paint.

Select a single-part polyurethane paint—white is the traditional color for painted bulkheads—and roll it on with a foam roller. If you are painting with white, or any light color, the roller will leave a slightly textured finish; tipping with a brush will be unnecessary, and perhaps even undesirable. Practice on a scrap of laminate or the laminate surface of a discarded kitchen cabinet or piece of furniture.

PLASTIC LAMINATES

Decorative plastic laminate (often called Formica after the best-known brand name) provides an excellent "coating" for flat (and some curved) surfaces, and it is used extensively in boats of all types and price ranges. It is a tough, durable material with a life-span measured not in years but decades. Plastic laminate is usually replaced or re-covered not because it has worn out (though it does fade) but because the owner wants a different color or pattern.

The long life of plastic laminate offers a challenge in its selection. Trendy patterns may look great this year and next, but in five years they will date your boat. Similarly, a countertop that just matches the fuchsia in your settee cushions may quickly lose its appeal when it comes time to reupholster. This is not to say you should always select neutral colors—five years of pizzazz beats twenty years of blah hands down—but make your selection with the knowledge that if you select wisely, you will do this only once.

There are other countertop materials—tile, stainless steel, Corian—but the durability, simplicity, and light weight of plastic laminate, combined with a nearly unlimited selection of colors and patterns, have made it the default choice for most galley counters. The laminate was originally applied to an underlay of plywood when your boat was constructed, and if you are building a counter from scratch, that is how you should do it. Most boatowners, however, will not be changing the counter, just the surface, and in this instance the new laminate is installed right over the old—the procedure detailed here.

Decorative laminate typically comes in horizontal grade ($\frac{1}{16}$-inch thick), tough enough to shrug off the hard use of countertops, and in vertical grade ($\frac{1}{32}$-inch), ideal for cabinet faces and bulkheads. A standard sheet is 4 feet by 8 feet, but 10-foot sheets are commonly available, and even larger sizes can be obtained. The sheet size you need is determined by the size of the counter—avoid any seams in the top if at all possible.

Plastic laminate on bulkheads is far more durable than paint. The traditional color for yacht bulkheads has long been white. The main reason for this is probably that white bulkheads give the confines of a cramped cabin a more spacious appearance. It also makes a tremendous difference in how light the cabin is, both in the daytime and with the cabin lights on at night. Because these benefits are so desirable, white bulkheads have never gone out of style. White bulkheads are hard to fault, and accented with wood trim, they give the interior of almost any boat the classic look of a fine yacht.

TOOLS

LAMINATE WORK requires a few special tools. Special saber-saw blades without any set to the teeth minimize chipping. A router fitted with a laminate-trimming bit makes short work of edge trimming. Use a file to trim edges with limited access. Tin snips will cut vertical grade laminate. Rough cut horizontal grade by scoring and breaking. A rubber roller helps ensure a secure bond.

CONTACT CEMENT FLAMABLE!

ACETONE

CHECKING FOR ADHESION OF THE OLD LAMINATE

The only precaution for installing new laminate over old is to make sure the bond between the old laminate and the plywood beneath it is still good.

This is rarely a problem, but if you find bond failure, the old laminate must be removed.

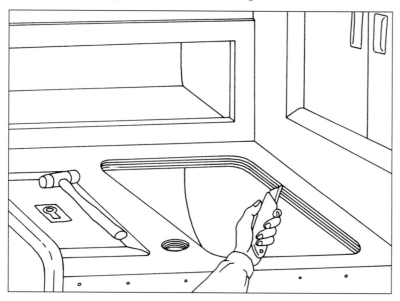

A sharpened drywall knife worked carefully between the laminate and the wood will usually lift the laminate with minimal damage to the wood. A heat gun can help anyplace the adhesion is still good.

If the surface looks okay, tap it with a plastic mallet or the handle of a screwdriver and listen for any sound differences that indicate bond failure. A bubble under the old laminate is an obvious failure. Check edges exposed by the removal of appliances or trim with the tip of a knife, but be careful not to chip the laminate; you are just checking to see if it is loose, not trying to loosen it.

DISK SANDING THE SURFACE

To give the new laminate a good bonding surface, thoroughly sand the old surface with 80-grit paper. This is one of the few instances in the curved environment of a boat where a belt sander can be used to advantage, but a disk sander will do the job just as well and is probably easier to handle.

Keep the sander moving in order not to introduce highs and lows. The *entire* surface must be uniformly dull: hand sand inside corners and any other areas inaccessible to the power sander. Fill any holes or surface damage with an epoxy filler, and sand the repairs smooth. Don't expect the laminate (especially vertical grade) to bridge voids; any significant underlying flaw will eventually print through.

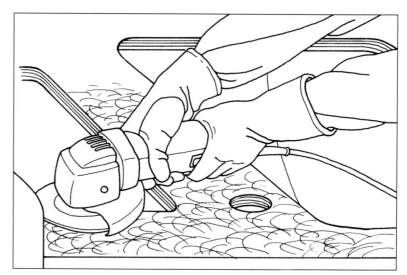

MAKING A PAPER PATTERN

New laminate can be cut from measurements, but with the irregular lines and angles of boat surfaces, the most foolproof method of sizing the laminate is with a paper pattern.

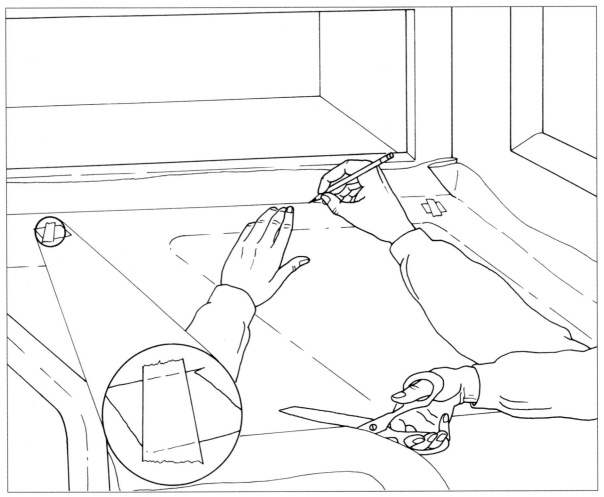

1 Lay the paper on the surface and carefully crease the paper into the intersections with other surfaces and over outside corners. It is usually a good idea to cut four holes in your pattern near the outside corners and run tape across these holes to hold the paper in position.

2 When the outline is complete, cut the paper on the lines, then check the cut pattern again for fit. Make any needed adjustments. Pattern shortages can be corrected by adding a piece of paper tape and trimming the tape to the correct shape. Once the pattern is perfect, write TOP on its surface while it is still in place to prevent any confusion later when you cut the laminate.

CUTTING THE NEW LAMINATE

It is a very good idea to practice cutting laminate on a scrap before you attempt to cut the pieces for installation. Cut horizontal grade with a saber saw fitted with a special laminate or plastics blade. Some laminates will cut perfectly while others will exhibit a tendency to chip. If you are using a variable-speed saw, try cutting at different speeds until you find the speed that leaves the cleanest edge. Always cut from the backside.

Vertical grade laminate can be cut with tin snips or heavy-duty scissors, but the laminate may tend to tear. Technique can usually avoid this, or at least force the tears into the cut-off side of the cut; practicing on a scrap is essential.

A quick way to rough-cut laminate is to score it on the good side with a special laminate-scoring tool or a razor knife, then break it like glass over a sharp edge. Again, practice is the key.

If all the edges of your laminate will be covered with trim, a chipped cut-line won't matter, and you can cut the piece the same size as your pattern. Where an edge of the laminate will show, that edge must be given extra width to allow for trim. Cutting 1/8 inch outside the pattern line is usually sufficient, but measure the depth of the largest chips on your test cut and allow more material if necessary.

Finished edges that cannot be trimmed after the laminate is installed—where the back of the counter butts against a cabinet, for example—will need to be finished before (see below). You can often avoid the need to do this by placing this edge of your pattern along an edge of the full sheet.

Mark the visible edges and the hidden edges (covered with trim) on your pattern, then place the visible edges along the finished edges of the sheet or allow extra material for trimming. Remember to orient the pattern correctly—you will be marking the backside of the laminate, so the TOP you wrote on the pattern should not be visible when you trace the pattern onto the laminate.

Always dry-fit the laminate to check the fit before applying any adhesive. If alignment will be required, align the piece now and put pencil guidemarks on the laminate and adjoining surfaces.

APPLYING THE CONTACT CEMENT

Glue plastic laminate in place with contact cement. Contact cement attaches to almost any surface when it is wet, but only to itself when it is dry. Use a throw-away brush to completely coat both the surface being covered and the back of the new laminate, then let the glue dry. One coat is usually sufficient, but if you are laminating over bare wood, a second coat may be required. The dry glue should leave the surface with a slight sheen. It is dry when no longer sticky to the touch (be sure you don't have glue on your finger).

For the marine environment, always select petroleum-based adhesive, never water-based. The right contact cement will have "Flammable" printed prominently on the label—and it is. Very! So be sure everything that might generate a spark or flame is off. Light a cigarette while using this stuff in the cabin, and at least you won't be a lung-cancer statistic.

Contact cement is also quite toxic, so apply it to the new laminate on deck. When coating surfaces that can't be taken on deck, be sure you have lots of ventilation, and as soon as you get the surface coated, get out of there until the glue dries. If you have an organic respirator—you're going to need one to paint the bottom—this is another good use for it.

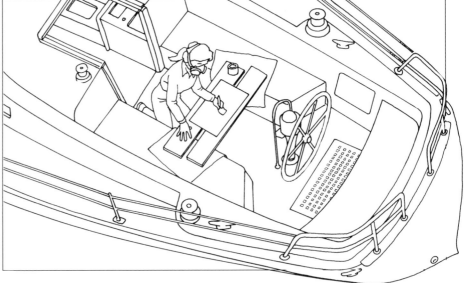

KEEPING THE GLUE-COATED SURFACES APART WHILE POSITIONING

Get two cement-coated surfaces too close and one will latch onto the other like a frog snapping up a fly—with the same opportunity for a second chance. Contact cement allows for zero adjustment once the surfaces touch. Avoid this potential disaster by covering one surface entirely with waxed paper—safe stix, so to speak.

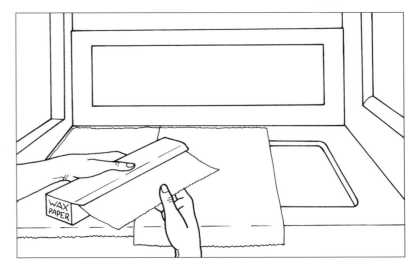

REMOVING THE SEPARATOR

With the help of the pencil marks you made when you did your dry-fit, position the new laminate on top of the paper. Holding the laminate in position with one hand, slide one of the end strips of paper out an inch or so. Press the laminate lightly in the area the paper uncovered (you can't see it, but you will know where it is) to fix the laminate in place. Now slide each of the other paper strips slightly; you just want to make sure you don't have any of them pinched behind the edge of the laminate while you can still lift it to free them.

If the papers are all free, check your alignment one more time. Working from the corner where the two pieces are already glued, extract the strips of paper one at a time and press the laminate down by sliding your hand across the top, always smoothing toward the area still separated by paper.

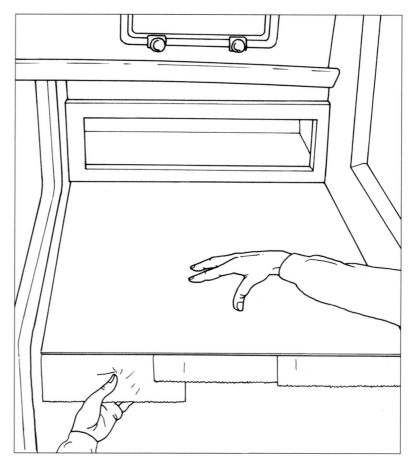

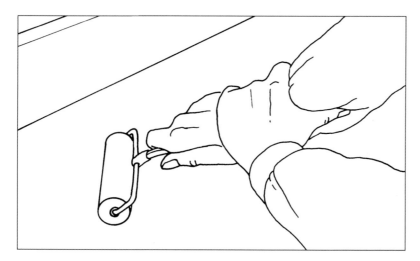

ROLLING A GOOD BOND

When all the paper separators are out, roll the surface firmly with a rubber roller to ensure full contact. Roll initially in a single direction to force any air pockets to the edge.

TRIMMING WITH A ROUTER OR A FILE

All the necessary trimming of a typical galley counter will take about two minutes with a router, so if you don't have one, buy or borrow one for this job. It makes it s-o-o-o easy.

If you need a finished edge before you install the laminate—the back edge of the counter, for example—clamp the laminate with a slight overhang to a straight piece of wood and run the router guide (the roller on the bottom of the bit) against the board. To have space at the ends for your clamps, rout the straight edge on the laminate before you cut out the piece.

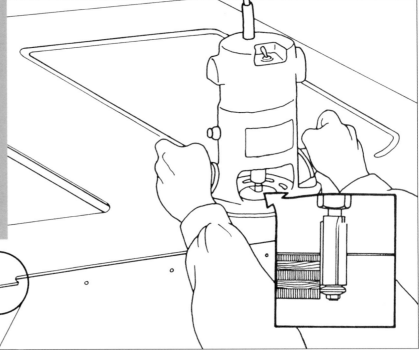

1 To trim sink openings and other interior cutouts, first drill a hole in the laminate over the counter opening large enough for the router bit. There is no need to saw out the opening; the router will cut out and trim in the same operation.

2 Use a file to trim where the router fails to reach. Lay the flat side of the file on the edge at a slight angle and use the edge of the file in a sawing motion to trim the laminate. If a router is unavailable, a file can be used for all the trimming.

REPLACING THE TRIM

If you want to be able to take the trim off easily in the future, reinstall it with finishing nails. Glue is more secure but infinitely harder to remove later without damage.

Since you drove the old nails through the trim, they are probably still in the furniture or bulkhead. Even if you pulled them out, the hole is still there; any nails used in these locations will have to be a size larger than the ones taken out. A better alternative is smaller nails in new holes.

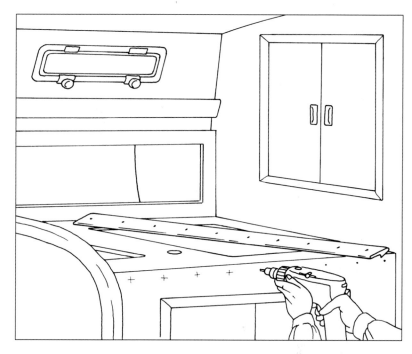

1 Nails will usually penetrate vertical-grade laminate without difficulty, but pilot holes may be needed to get a slender finishing nail through horizontal grade. If you cannot find a bit smaller than the nails you are using, give each nail a good rap to mark its location on the laminate, then set the trim aside and drill *through the laminate only* at the marked locations.

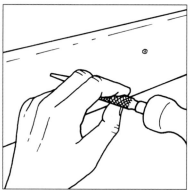

2 Set the nails below the surface with a nail set, then fill the holes—new and old—with a little wood putty.

3 Sand the patches and apply the finish of your choice to the trim.

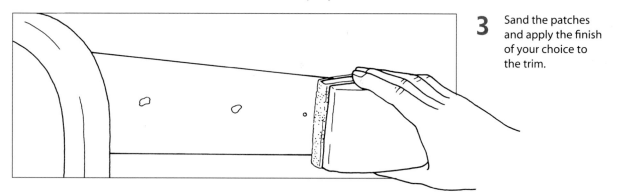

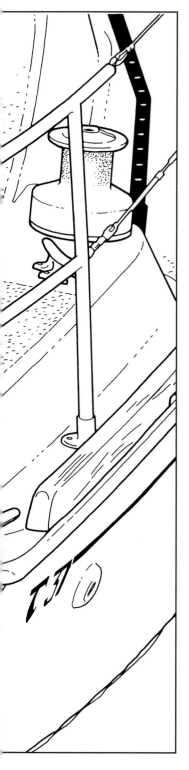

WOOD FINISHES

On modern fiberglass pleasure boats, exposed wood is there primarily to enhance the boat's appearance. Of course, teak handrails do serve the necessary function of providing a secure handhold, but we could accomplish the same thing with stainless steel rails and eliminate most maintenance in the bargain. So why don't we see more sailboats with stainless handrails? Because we want that warm, traditional look that only wood can provide.

We also like the look of wood in the cabin, at the very least as accent trim to give the interior a yachty look. Below deck almost any attractive wood will serve, although teak is by far the most popular. Teak reigns on the deck as well.

The second most common trim wood is mahogany, prized for its tight grain, classic color, and spectacular beauty when covered with a dozen coats of carefully applied varnish. To survive, mahogany must be protected from the elements.

Teak, on the other hand, can be left untreated for years, even decades, without losing integrity, which makes this wood consistent with the low maintenance nature of fiberglass boats. High oil content makes good quality teak virtually impervious to the marine environment, but while its integrity may survive neglect, its appearance is certain to suffer.

It is true that good teak left untreated should weather to an attractive ash gray, but the assault of modern-day air pollutants soon turn neglected teak nearly black. Scrubbing tends to leave behind an unattractive mottled look, neither golden nor gray. Most boatowners eventually find themselves unhappy with either look and decide that some treatment is essential. Some simply paint all exposed wood brown, an eminently pragmatic course, but if you want the natural beauty of the wood to show, you must apply a clear coating. For mahogany (and almost all other woods), varnish is the only practical choice. For teak the choices are oil, sealer, or varnish.

OILING WOOD TRIM

The application of oil has long been a common method of bringing out the natural beauty of wood. Oil intensifies the colors and grain patterns of wood, and gives the wood a rich, warm appearance. Because it simply enhances the inherent beauty of the wood—more like salt than sauce—oiling is arguably the most attractive of all wood finishes.

Virtually any uncoated wood surface can be oiled, but if the wood will be exposed to the elements, oiling is likely to prove unsatisfactory. Oil is the least durable common wood finish, and only naturally oily woods will tolerate the minimal pro-tection of oiling. Aboard a boat, that means teak.

Oiling teak on boats is a time-honored tradition, and oiling does restore some of the teak's natural oils and resins. However, the benefit of oiling exterior teak is extremely transitory. The irritating truth is that teak will last just as long if you don't oil it—longer really, since repeated between-coat scrubbing wears the wood away. But oiling teak isn't about protecting the wood; it's about recovering and maintaining that golden glow that made us want teak on the boat in the first place. You can set a party table with tarnished silver, too, but it's not so attractive.

SCRUBBING TEAK

Before teak can be oiled (or given any other coating, for that matter), it must be completely clean. Use the mildest cleaner that does the job. Start with a 75/25 mixture of liquid detergent and chlorine bleach (no water), boosted with TSP. Apply with a stiff brush, scrubbing lightly with the grain. Leave the mixture on the wood for several minutes to give the detergent time to suspend the dirt, and the bleach time to lighten the wood, then rinse thoroughly by flooding and brushing.

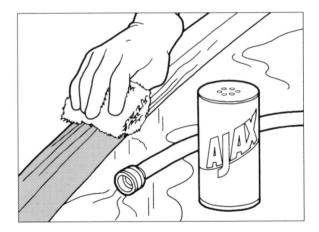

LIGHTENING THE COLOR

If the scrubbed teak is dark or stained when it dries, a cleaner with oxalic acid is required. This is the active ingredient in most single-part teak cleaners. It is also the bleaching agent in Ajax scouring powder—that ubiquitous blue can under the kitchen sink. Expect teak cleaner targeted for boat use to cost 10 times the price of lowly Ajax (biting the hand that feeds); judge for yourself if it is 10 times better. Whichever you select, brush the cleaner onto wet teak and give it time to work, then scrub the wood with Scotchbrite or bronze wool. (Never, ever, *ever* use steel wool aboard your boat—it will leave a trail of rust freckles that will be impossible to remove.) Oxalic acid will dull paint and fiberglass, so wet down surrounding surfaces before you start and keep them free of the cleaner. Rinse the scrubbed wood thoroughly—brushing is required—and let it dry completely.

USING A TWO-PART TEAK CLEANER

Two-part teak cleaners are dramatically effective at restoring the color to soiled, stained, and neglected teak, but these formulations contain a strong acid—usually hydrochloric—and should only be used when all other cleaning methods have failed.

Use a nylon-bristle brush to apply two-part cleaner. If you use a natural-bristle brush, the cleaner will dissolve the bristles; it is doing the same thing to your teak.

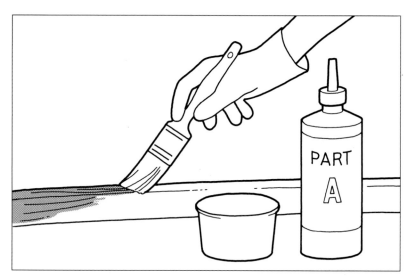

1 Wet the wood to be cleaned, then paint part 1 (or A) onto the wet wood, avoiding contact with adjoining surfaces.

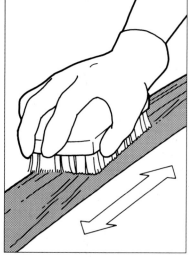

2 Scrub with the grain.

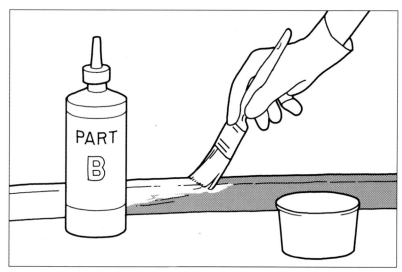

3 Part 2 (or B) neutralizes the acid in part 1 and usually has some cleaning properties. Paint sufficient part 2 onto the teak to get a uniform color change. Scrub lightly.

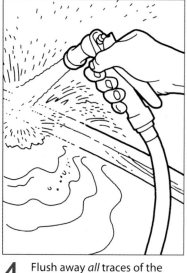

4 Flush away *all* traces of the cleaner and let the wood dry.

APPLYING TEAK OIL

Teak oils are primarily either linseed oil or tung oil, bolstered by resins to make them more durable. Linseed oil tends to darken the teak, but it is significantly cheaper. Tung oil doesn't darken the wood, and it is more water-resistant than linseed oil—a notable advantage for boat use. However, a month or two after application, it may be hard to discern that much difference since both oils carbonize in the sun and turn dark. Proprietary teak oils address this problem with various additives, including pigments, UV filters, and mildew retardants. Some that perform admirably in one climate are reviled in another. If you are going to oil your teak, make your teak-oil selection based on the recommendations of other boatowners in your area.

The best way to apply teak oil is to brush it on. Thinning the first coat about 20 percent with mineral spirits or turpentine will encourage the oil to penetrate the wood more deeply. *Immediately* wipe away (with a spirits-dampened cloth) any drips or runs on fiberglass or painted surfaces; otherwise the resins the oil contains will leave dark, nearly-impossible-to-remove stains. Watch out for sneaky runs below the rail.

Oiling requires multiple coats. The teak will initially "drink" the oil, but by the third coat, oil will begin to stand in some areas. Wipe up excess oil with a cloth. Continue to brush on the oil, and wipe away any excess until the wood is saturated. The wood should have a matte finish without any shiny spots.

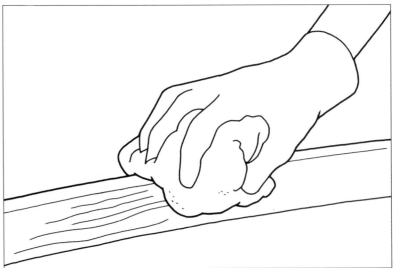

WIPING INTERIOR WOOD SURFACES WITH LEMON OIL

1 Wash unvarnished interior wood surfaces with 1 cup of *liquid* household laundry detergent and 1 cup of chlorine bleach in 1 gallon of water. Use a towel—not too wet or you will raise the grain—and leave the solution on the wood for 30 minutes to kill mildew spores. Rinse thoroughly with fresh water and a clean towel. If the grain is raised, sand the wood with 120-grit sandpaper on an orbital sander, then remove all surface dust with a mineral-spirits-*dampened* cloth. (Raised grain should happen only once; after you oil the wood, the oil will shield the wood from water penetration the next time you wash it.)

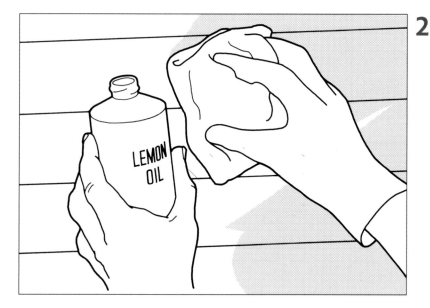

2 Use lemon oil on interior woods; it feeds the wood, is waxy rather than sticky when it dries, and is poison to mildew. Rub the oil into the grain of uncoated interior wood surfaces with a soft cloth. After a week, give the wood a second application, then oil it every two or three months after that, or as the wood needs it.

SEALERS

Sealers are another approach to achieving the natural look. Sealers don't feed the wood but, as the name suggests, they seal in natural oils and resins, seal out moisture and dirt. You can concoct an effective sealer by thinning spar varnish 50 percent with mineral spirits. Sealers work fine on new wood—if the seal is maintained by regularly applying a fresh coat—but on old wood the oils and resins you are trying to seal in have, like Elvis, already left the premises.

Some commercial teak products blend oil and sealer in an effort to combine the rejuvenating characteristics of the one with the durability of the other. These products are often called "dressings" or "treatments," and some enjoy substantial popularity.

PREPARING OLD WOOD

The first step toward applying a sealer on old wood is the same as for any finish—thoroughly clean the wood and brighten (bleach) it to a uniform color. Next, lost oils must be restored by oiling the wood until it refuses to accept more. Then take a break—*for a couple of weeks*. The resins need to dry before you apply the sealer.

When you return, wash the wood; the fresh oil has been snagging grime for a fortnight. When the wood is dry, wipe it heavily with a rag soaked in acetone to remove all oil from the surface. Yes, you did just put that oil on there, but the sealer needs an oil-free surface to get a grip. The oil the wood has absorbed is unaffected by this quick-flashing solvent.

APPLYING A SEALER

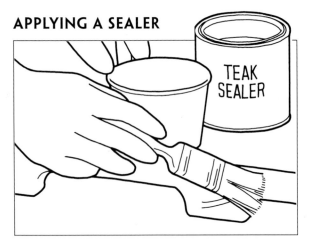

1 Apply sealer exactly like oil. A throw-away brush is adequate for the job, and brushing technique is not a concern.

2 Wipe away all excess with a cloth. Apply additional coats—wet on wet—until the wiped surface shows a uniform matte finish.

VARNISHING: PREPARATION

Varnish has long been the brightwork finish of choice among the yachting set. A mirror-like coating of varnish on tight-grained mahogany attracts universal admiration—for the boat and, by extension, for her owner. Skillfully applied and properly maintained, varnish is second only to high-gloss hull coatings in its ability to transform a boat from peasant to queen.

Aside from its much-admired appearance, varnish offers genuine protection for the wood. Wood coated with varnish will not dry out and split, will not absorb moisture and rot, is unaffected by dirt and pollution, and will be untouched, thus unstained, by oily or greasy spills. Protected from the sun, varnish will last indefinitely; even with direct sun exposure, varnish will outlast oils and sealers by at least a factor of five.

For exterior application, select spar varnish, not urethane varnish. Urethane varnish provides a harder, more abrasion-resistant surface, which makes it an excellent choice for interior woodwork, but it tends to lose its grip on the wood when subjected to continuous sun exposure. Because the finish is a thin layer of plastic, it may be that it is susceptible to a "greenhouse" effect, condensing moisture on its underside, which hydraulically lifts the coating. Whatever the cause, the adhesion of urethane varnish applied on exterior wood is almost certain to fail sooner rather than later, and the varnish will peel away in plastic-wrap-like sheets.

The absence of pigment in varnish means it does not shield the underlying surface the way paint does. The sun penetrates the coating and carbonizes the oils in the wood, causing the wood to darken *beneath* the varnish. To minimize this effect, varnish makers add ultraviolet inhibitors—sun screens—to their products. For exterior brightwork, select a quality spar varnish heavily fortified with UV inhibitors. As always, get local recommendations from other boatowners before selecting a specific varnish.

If the wood you intend to varnish has been previously varnished, and the old varnish is in bad shape, you will have to strip it. (If the varnish is in good condition—fat chance—skip to "'Laying On' the Finish Coats.") Sanding away the old varnish can be frustrating because the friction-heated varnish tends to soften and gum up the paper. The cleanest, safest, and sometimes the easiest way to strip old varnish is with a cabinet scraper. If you develop your skill with a cabinet scraper, you will be amazed at how smooth it leaves the wood.

STRIPPING OLD VARNISH

1 Hold a sharpened 4- or 5-inch cabinet scraper (see "Sharpening a Scraper" on page 31) tilted toward you at about 75° to the wood and draw it toward you. The microscopic burr on the edge of the scraper will finely plane the surface. Keep drawing the scraper across the wood until all the varnish has been planed off.

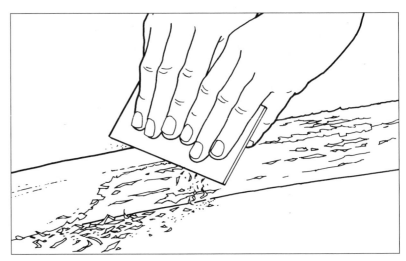

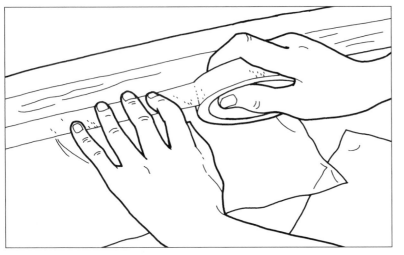

2 A chemical stripper can take much of the work out of removing old varnish, but the stripper will also lift paint, and many can damage gelcoat. Mask all surrounding surfaces, using sheet plastic, not newspaper. Select the thickest stripper you can find—so it will stay where you want it.

3 Pour a little into a small open container, not directly onto the wood. Dip a throw-away brush into the stripper, but do not unload it. Apply *with a single stroke*, probably not longer than 4 inches. Dip and apply the next 4 inches, and so on. Vapors from the stripper do the work, and if you brush back and forth, you release them into the air and reduce the effectiveness of the stripper by *as much as 80 percent*! Direct sun also reduces the stripper's effectiveness by drying it prematurely .

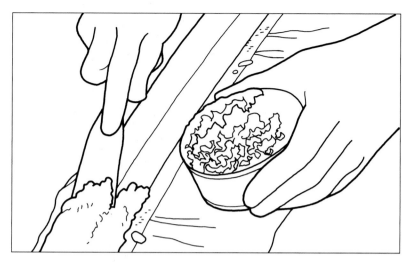

4 Leave the stripper on the varnish for about 30 minutes, then use a wide putty knife to scrape off the softened varnish. Be careful not to gouge the wood or raise a splinter. Don't let any of the curls fall onto painted or gel-coated surfaces. Wipe the toxic scrapings into an empty paint bucket for later disposal.

5 Scrub the wood with bronze wool to remove the varnish in curved or irregular areas and to clear the grain. If some varnish remains, apply the stripper a second time. After the second application has been scraped and scrubbed, use a cabinet scraper to remove any varnish "islands" and to fair the surface.

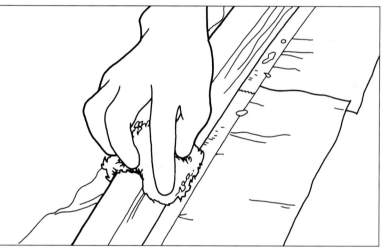

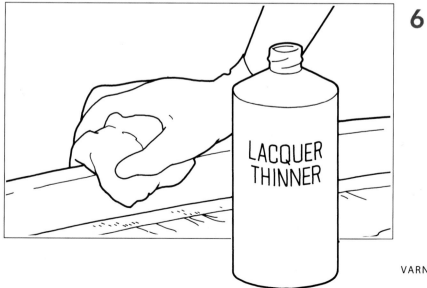

6 Wipe away all traces of stripper and varnish residue with a cloth soaked in denatured alcohol or lacquer thinner.

LACQUER THINNER

BLEACHING RAW WOOD

For varnishing to succeed, the underlying wood must have a uniform color. Where old varnish has been gouged and split or allowed to peel, the wood will have taken on multi-hues. Chemical stripping is almost certain to leave the wood mottled. Scraping and sanding may restore uniform color, but only if a substantial amount of wood is removed. Unvarnished wood will also show a patchwork of discolorations from stains and mildew.

Mild discoloration may respond to scrubbing with a powdered cleaner—Ajax or your favorite single-part teak cleaner. (Note that most two-part cleaners cannot be used on woods other than teak.) After you scrub the wood, if it still shows stains or multiple shades, it will need to be bleached.

For this bleaching, you need oxalic acid, which you can buy in crystal form at your local hardware store. Also buy a box of soda ash or borax to use as a neutralizer.

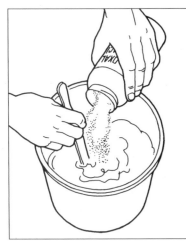

1 To make the bleach solution, stir oxalic-acid crystals into warm water until they stop dissolving. A strong solution requires about 16 ounces of oxalic acid to a gallon of water.

2 Paint or sponge this solution onto the wood, taking great care not to get it onto any other surface—it will etch paint and gelcoat.

3 Let it dry completely, then vacuum away the powder that remains, or brush it carefully into a dustpan.

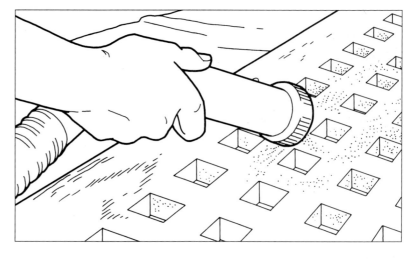

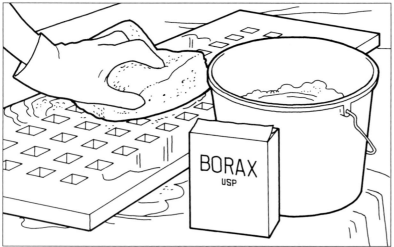

4 Mix a cup of soda ash or borax into a 2½-gallon bucket of water and wet the bleached wood generously with this solution.

5 Hose the wood and surrounding surfaces thoroughly, scrubbing the wood with a soft brush.

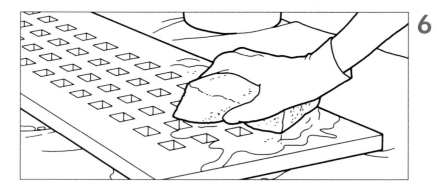

6 Treat the wood a second time with the neutralizing solution, then energetically flood and scrub again.

  The wood should dry to a uniform color. Remaining dark spots can be retreated, but it may be difficult to achieve consistency by spot-bleaching.

SURFACE PREPARATION

Before you varnish, you want the wood surface to be as smooth as possible. Previously unvarnished wood is likely to be quite rough. Bleached wood may also have a ridged surface because the acid eats away the softer wood cells. Regardless of whether the wood is weathered, bleach-damaged, or new, sanding is required.

Scrub and perhaps bleach the wood first to remove dirt and other contaminants from the grain and to brighten the color of the wood.

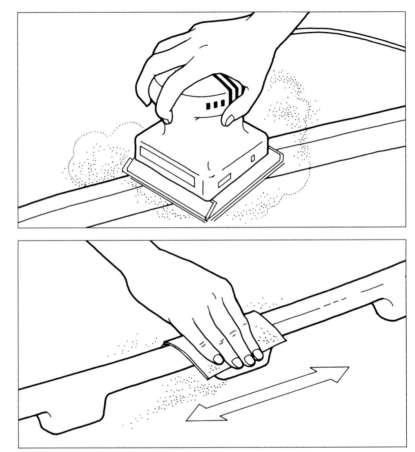

Sand rough wood with an orbital sander loaded with 80- or 100-grit aluminum-oxide paper.

Anywhere you have to hand sand, be sure to sand with the grain; scratches across the grain will show through the varnish.

If the wood has been bleached, the sanding dust may still harbor some acid, so hose the wood after sanding to thoroughly rinse it away. This may raise the grain again, which will require another application of sandpaper.

Unless the wood is teak, switch to a finer grit for the final pass. The oiliness of teak makes it difficult for the varnish to adhere, so finish sanding with 100-grit paper provides a better "tooth" and con-tributes to a longer-lasting finish. On other woods—mahogany, for example—150-grit paper will yield a slightly better finish. Use an even finer grit on interior furniture—120-grit for teak and 220-grit for other woods.

After sanding, use a rag dampened with mineral spirits, turning it often, to wipe away all the sanding dust. When the wood is ivory smooth and dust free, you are ready to varnish.

VARNISHING: THE INITIAL COATS

To achieve its mirror-like finish, varnish must fill the grain of the wood, requiring the varnish to be relatively viscous. This is a desirable characteristic in later coats, but initially this viscosity prevents the varnish from penetrating the wood. The varnish bridges the pores of the wood, trapping air and finish-lifting moisture in the tiny voids.

To avoid this situation, thin the first two or three coats with mineral spirits, turpentine, or the thinner recommended by the varnish manufacturer. The first coat should be thinned by 50 percent, i.e., ½ ounce of thinner for every ounce of varnish. Thinning allows the varnish to fully penetrate the wood, effectively converting the varnish into a sealer. Applying a sealer other than thinned varnish as a base coat is not a good idea since these products often give the varnish an off color.

WHEN TO VARNISH

Although less so than they used to be, today's marine varnishes are still sensitive to moisture and temperature, especially in the first two hours after application. You will have to wait until the morning dew evaporates (oddly enough, hosing dew-soaked wood will cause it to dry sooner), and you want to finish well before the moisture settles again in the evening. Don't varnish on a day when the humidity meter is pegged at 100 percent. If rain is threatening or conditions are right for fog, put this job off for another day.

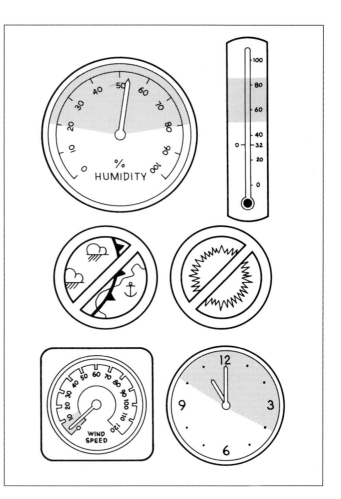

The varnish flows better if it is warm, so on a cool day, place the can in the sun or in a pan of warm water (open the can lid slightly). On the other hand, cool varnish will give you more time to brush it out, so chilling it on a hot day can be just as beneficial. Generally a warm surface is desirable, but too much sun can cook the varnish—if you need shade, so does the varnish.

A sudden temperature change during the critical two hours will cloud the varnish, so check the weather map for approaching fronts before you start. Red sky in the morning, varnisher take warning.

BUBBLES—THE NEMESIS

1 Varnish should always be applied with as few brush strokes as possible to minimize the number of bubbles introduced into the finish. For the same reason, never shake varnish, and if stirring is necessary—to add thinner, for example—stir slowly and gently.

2 Always pour varnish through a fine-mesh paint filter (or a double layer of pantyhose) before you use it, even if the can is new. Never apply varnish directly from its can; decant the amount you will be using into a clean container. Cleaning the rim with your brush and wiping the varnish back into the can introduces bubbles and bits of dried varnish; use a rag or paper towel to clean the rim, and reseal the can immediately.

paint filter

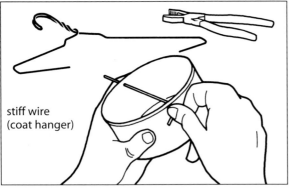

stiff wire (coat hanger)

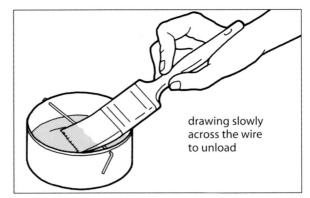

drawing slowly across the wire to unload

3 A tuna-can-size container limits the air exposure of the varnish before it is applied. Unload your brush on a wire rather than the curved rim of the container to minimize bubbles.

4 Dip the brush tip —not more than ⅓ of the bristles—long enough to become saturated. If not fully saturated, the brush will lay on bubbles rather than varnish. Unload one side of the brush.

TIP: Wipe both sides of the brush on a second can *after* each varnish application to expel particles, loose bristles, and dust.

BRUSHING TECHNIQUE

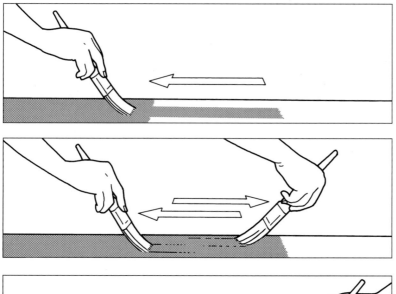

Six or more coats will be necessary to achieve the foot-deep finish potential of varnish. Apply the first coats quickly and without fuss. A throw-away brush—as long as it shows no tendency to shed bristles—is adequate for the first three or four coats. A foam brush can also be used with thinned varnish. Some find that for later coats foam brushes hold too little unthinned varnish, but foam brushes NEVER leave a bristle in the finish and they can lay down a stroke-free finish.

The wood will change color when you apply the first coat, but most of the varnish will be absorbed. As soon as the initial coat is dry to the touch, apply a second coat thinned about 25 percent. Allow both coats to dry overnight.

SANDING BETWEEN COATS

It is possible to apply multiple coats of varnish without sanding between coats. As long as you apply each coat within the recoat time specified on the can, the solvent in the varnish softens the previous coat and allows for a molecular bond. But for the smoothest finish, sanding between coats is required.

After the initial coats, sand each coat with 180-grit paper (220-grit for interior furniture). Use an orbital sander on large areas, keeping the sander moving to avoid softening the varnish. Small areas can be hand sanded, using a block if the surface is flat. Sanding not only removes all surface roughness and blemishes, it also provides essential tooth for the next coat. Never apply varnish (or paint, for that matter) to a glossy surface unless you are within the recoat time.

keep moving

KEEPING THE SURFACE DUST-FREE

Remove all dust from the varnished surface after sanding by wiping the surface with a spirits-dampened cloth or a tack rag (see sidebar). Preventing dust and other contaminants from spoiling the surface *after* you apply the coat is somewhat more challenging.

Wash the dust from all surrounding surfaces if you can do so without wetting the wood; otherwise wipe up the dust with a wet towel. Apply varnish on a still day. Applying it at anchor well away from shore has much to recommend it. In a slip, wet the dock and proximate shore to hold down dust. If the boat is on land, wet the ground around it.

Below deck, remove cushions and all other dust generators. Damp-wipe all interior surfaces, and mist—with a spritzer bottle—any fabric surfaces you cannot remove. Also mist your clothes.

TACK RAG

TACK RAGS ARE READILY available from hardware and paint stores, but for varnish work they can sometimes introduce contaminants. Make your own with a clean cotton cloth soaked in warm water and wrung out. Sprinkle the cloth with turpentine, followed with about a spoonful of your varnish. Wring the cloth again to distribute the varnish. Store it in a Ziploc bag between uses.

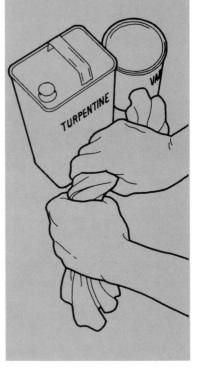

THE THIRD AND FOURTH COATS

For the third coat, thin the varnish just 10 percent, and apply this coat, like the first two, with minimal ado. Allow it to dry overnight, then sand the surface.

The fourth coat is the first one you apply without thinning the varnish and the last of the preparatory coats. Consider all coats after the fourth as finish coats, and take greater care in their application.

"LAYING ON" THE FINISH COATS

1 Applying the finish coats of varnish should be more like writing than painting. You do not want to worry the varnish with a lot of brush strokes. Think more of old-fashioned ink pens, the kind you have to dip in the ink. When you apply the nib to the paper, if you move it too slow, the ink stains the paper in ugly blobs; if you move it too fast, the line thins and skips. When you get the right speed and the right pressure, the pen rewards you with a sharp, crisp, perfect line. And the varnish brush correctly drawn rewards you with a flawless, glassy finish.

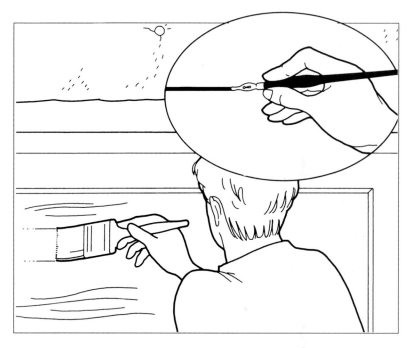

2 For the fifth coat, dip the tip of the brush in fresh unthinned varnish. This is the time to get out your good badger-hair or ox-hair brush. Unload one side on the wire, then apply the varnish with a single stroke, loaded side of the brush against the wood. Use another stroke or two—touching the surface lightly and drawing the brush slowly—to distribute the varnish. Apply each brush-load a few inches in front of the previous application, drawing the inital stroke back into the wet edge.

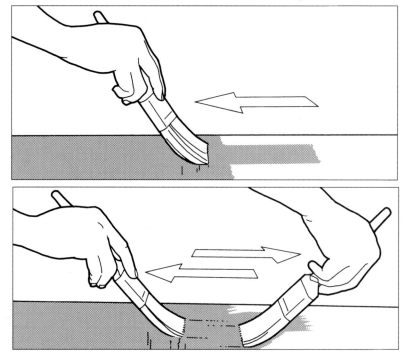

3 Finish with a single long stroke, or parallel strokes if the area is wider than your brush. Begin this final stroke just inside the old "wet edge," which is where the previous brush-load of varnish ended, and draw evenly beyond the new wet edge—where the varnish you just applied ends. If you brush back into the previous application, the technique usually recommended, excess varnish is pushed back into the previous application, causing a ridge or a wave in the finish; brushing out of the previous application moves excess varnish forward. In order not to mark the varnish where you start your final stroke, start the forward motion of your brush well before where you want the stroke to begin, and with the lightest of touches, "land" the brush—like landing an airplane—just behind the edge of your latest application.

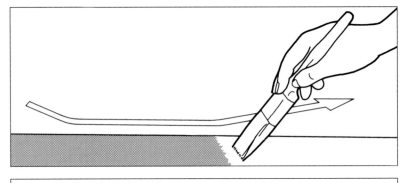

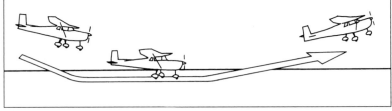

And so on, and so on. Before you return the brush to the varnish, wipe both sides on the edge of an empty can to remove contaminants. Dip the tip and apply the next brush load, beginning just at the wet edge. Distribute with a stroke or two, and finish with a light stroke from old wet edge to new. Continue, working quickly but drawing the brush slowly, until the surface is fully coated.

THE LAST COAT

The sixth coat is probably the final one. After the fifth coat is dry (at least overnight), sand it to remove any mistakes—runs, sags, or brush marks—and to provide smooth, uniform surface for the last coat. Some craftsmen elect not to use sandpaper before the last coat, scuffing the surface with fine bronze wool instead. Wipe the wood and all surrounding surfaces absolutely dust-free, and take all precautions against airborne dust—including waiting for another day if the wind is blowing. For the best possible finish, open a new can of varnish for the final coat.

Apply the sixth coat exactly like the previous one, only without the mistakes.

MAINTAINING A VARNISHED SURFACE

1 Before you put away the varnish, obtain a nail polish or a paste bottle—a bottle with a brush built into the lid—and after thoroughly cleaning it, funnel it full of fresh varnish. Tear a half-sheet of 220-grit sandpaper into six squares and rubber band them to the bottle. This is your first-aid kit. Keep it handy, and use it to immediately repair any nicks and scratches.

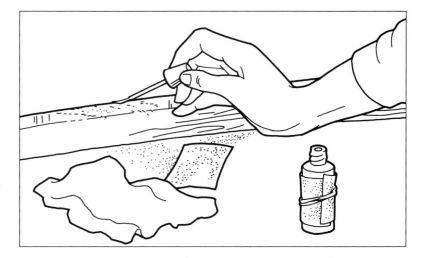

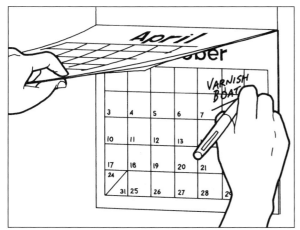

2 If you maintain the seal, varnish can last indefinitely. Besides avoiding moisture penetration at nicks and scratches, you must protect against surface erosion by periodically applying a fresh top coat. Exposed exterior varnish should be recoated at least annually in northern climes, every six months in the tropics. Scrub the varnish to remove all traces of grease and dirt, then sand the surface with 180-grit paper (or scuff it with bronze wool) and lay on a new finish coat.

3 The bond of the varnish is also damaged by the sun, and while the periodic addition of a fresh coat renews the UV protection of the varnish, the best protection is to cover the varnish; varnish kept mostly covered will last a decade or more.

BELOW THE WATERLINE

About half the exterior surface of the typical sailboat is under water. In many ways it is this underwater portion that faces the worst assault. Scores of organisms that live in the water find the broad, smooth expanse of a boat's bottom irresistible for setting up housekeeping. Left unprotected, the bottom soon becomes, at best, a carpet of grass or, at worst, a boat-shaped living reef. Neither condition is conducive to sparkling sailing performance.

The universal solution is to paint the underwater surfaces with antifouling bottom paint. The type of bottom paint you should use depends on whether your boat goes fast or slow, whether it is kept in the water or out, whether it stays in the water year-round or only for a few months, whether you race or cruise, what material your hull is constructed of, and perhaps your environmental leanings. The brand of paint that will give the best results depends on what kind of critters lurk in your local waters. Consult the "Understanding Paints" section of this book to determine the best type. To select the best brand, consult other boatowners in your area to determine the local favorite.

Unfortunately it isn't just the critters in the water that are attracted to your hull; it can be the water itself. Some fiberglass boats left in the water for a long period of time absorb significant amounts of water. Besides making the boat heavier, the water can combine with chemicals left over from the layup process to produce blisters and to form a destructive acidic solution.

The treatment is to let the hull dry out, then to replace or reinforce the gelcoat with a more water-impermeable barrier. A number of specialized coatings have come on the market in the last few years specifically for this purpose.

How much barrier coating or bottom paint do you need? Calculate a rough estimate of a boat's wetted area by multiplying the length times the beam times 0.90. The label will specify the coverage per gallon.

ANTIFOULING BOTTOM COATINGS

PREPARING THE BOTTOM FOR RECOATING

1 Assuming you are painting the bottom in a boatyard, the yard will pressure wash the hull for you immediately after it comes out of the water. This is usually included in the haul-out fee, but even if it isn't, be sure this happens. Most of the slime and vegetation will wash right off while still moist, but if they are allowed to dry, it will take a chisel to remove them—no exaggeration. Most yards also quickly scrape off barnacle encrustations as a part of the pressure-cleaning process.

2 If the old coat of bottom paint is in good condition and compatible with the new, all that is required is surface preparation. The safest and most environmentally friendly way to do this is to scrape it. Scraping peels away the old, dead paint without raising any dust, and the scrapings can easily be caught on plastic spread on the ground beneath the work area. Use a 2- or 3-inch hook scraper—any wider will bridge the curvature of the hull—and draw it toward you with sufficient pressure to peel the surface of the paint. Scraping is especially effective on softer bottom paints. Sharpen the scraper blade by drawing a mill file across the edge and chasing the edge with a whetstone; do not burnish a burr onto the edge of a hook scraper.

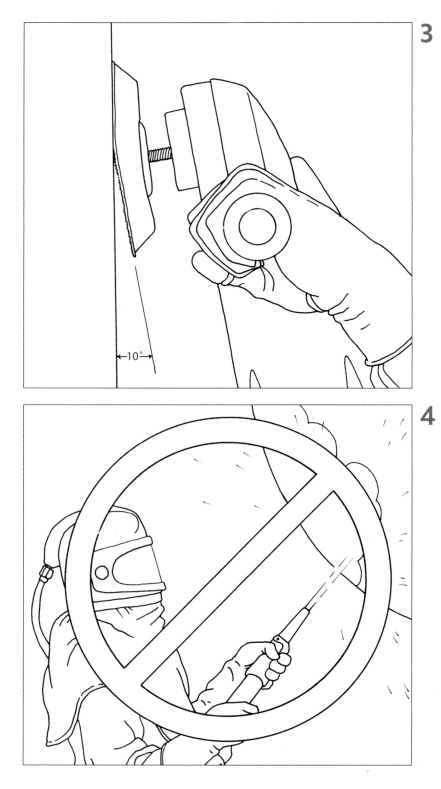

3 If scraping proves ineffective, as it may on hard bottom paints, sanding will be the next choice. A disk sander fitted with a foam pad and 80-grit paper will quickly and efficiently prepare a bottom for recoating. Tilt the sander about 10° so that only one side of the spinning disk is in contact with the surface. The direction of the tilt will depend on where you want the dust to fly. This dust is highly toxic, so wear a tight-fitting respirator—not a bandanna or a paper mask. There is no reason to sand the old paint away; sand it just enough to give you a clean, smooth surface for the new paint.

4 If the old paint needs to be removed entirely for reasons of compatibility, thickness, or loss of adhesion, sanding it all off is an arduous and messy job, and the cloud of toxic dust you will generate is probably illegal under the 1990 *Clean Air Act*. Your boatyard is likely to prohibit heavy sanding. They may suggest sandblasting. *Never* allow the hull of a fiberglass boat to be sandblasted, no matter how convincing the yard's argument. Sandblasting will make your gelcoat porous, virtually guaranteeing hull blisters later on, and if the operator is only slightly inattentive, the underlying laminate will also be damaged. If you have a steel hull, sandblast it all you want, but never on a plastic hull.

USING PEEL-TYPE STRIPPER

The easiest way to entirely strip old paint is with a chemical stripper, but great caution is required. The health hazards have already been mentioned. In addition, there is very little chemical difference between paint and gelcoat, meaning that most strippers will also attack the gelcoat beneath the paint. Those specifically formulated for use on fiberglass can be used with significantly less risk to the underlying gelcoat, *provided they are not left on the surface any longer than the recommended time—usually 15 minutes or less.* Lose track of the time—easy to do—and your gelcoat will suffer damage.

A better alternative is a so-called "safe stripper." These products contain no methylene chloride. They are just as effective as other strippers, but may require much longer to do the job. Peel Away, for example, should be left on the surface as long as 48 hours. Magi-Sol, another methylene-chlorideless stripper, requires at least two hours to work.

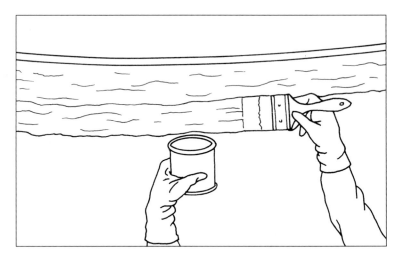

1 Paint the stripper onto the bottom paint. If you are using a methylene-chloride stripper, set a timer to make sure you can remove the stripper within the recommended exposure time.

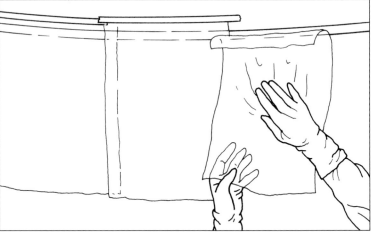

2 Strippers that call for extended exposure times can benefit from covering them to prevent the stripper from drying out and to trap all vapors against the paint. If covering sheets aren't provided, use plastic wrap or cut sections of plastic drop-cloth material.

3 Scrape away the lifted paint with a hook scraper, capturing the scrapings for proper disposal on a drop cloth spread under the work area. For methylene-chloride strippers, *immediately* wash the stripped area. (To avoid diluting the stripper, be sure the next area of application is a dry portion of the hull.)

FAIRING AND MINOR BLISTER REPAIR

Before you paint, repair any scratches, gouges, or hollows in the hull to make the surface fair. A few blisters in the gelcoat is no cause for alarm, but all blisters should be repaired as soon as they are discovered. Instructions for repairing more extensive hull damage can be found in *Sailboat Hull and Deck Repair* in this series.

1 Open the blister completely with a sharp tool and let it drain. A countersink bit on a power drill is an easy-to-control tool for opening blisters. Wear eye protection—the pressure beneath the blister can be more than twice that in a champagne bottle. Wipe it out with a rag soaked in **brush cleaner**—a water-soluble toluene-based product available at any hardware store.

2 Use a 36-grit disk on your disk sander to grind the blister into a shallow depression. The hollow should be 20 times as wide as it is deep, and it should be only as deep as required to remove any damaged laminate beneath the gelcoat. Grind scratches or gouges into a uniform V–shaped depression.

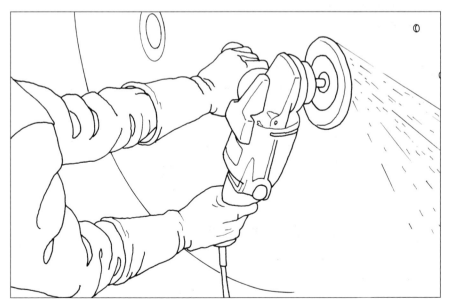

3 Scrub the depression squeaky clean with a hot TSP solution and a brush. Rinse fervently, then allow the spot to dry for a couple of days.

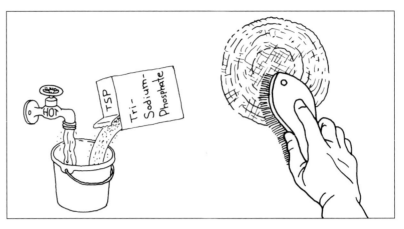

4 Paint the blister with unthickened epoxy, then fill it, if it is shallow, with epoxy resin thickened with colloidal silica to peanut butter consistency. Fill gouges and other surface damage the same way.

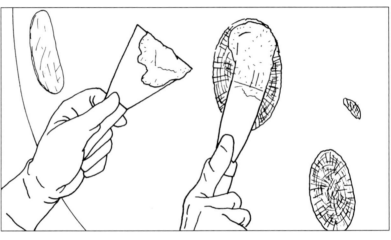

5 Deep depressions require layup of cloth disks of increasing diameter (never use mat with epoxy). Mask the hull, then paint the cavity with catalyzed epoxy. Saturate the first four disks and press each into place. Use the brush to compact them and remove excess resin. After the resin kicks—that is, begins to harden—apply additional layers (if needed) in exactly the same manner. For best results, use a squeegee or a short roller to make sure all the bubbles are forced from the laminates. Stop the layup at the bottom surface of the old gelcoat.

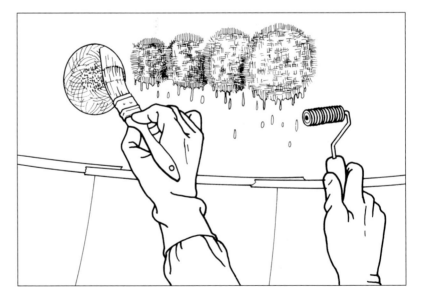

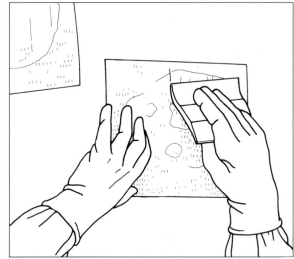

6 When the resin has kicked, finish filling the depression with silica-thickened epoxy. Take pains to get the surface as fair as possible, because the cured filler will resist sanding.

7 For smoother results, squeegee peel ply—a coated fabric epoxy does not adhere to—over the repair. The waxy amine blush will peel away with the peel ply when the epoxy has cured. If you don't use peel ply, scrub the epoxy surface with Scotchbrite and water before painting.

MIXING BOTTOM PAINT

Because the copper tends to settle into a solid lump in the bottom of the can, bottom paints generally require vigorous mixing. To allow stirring with the requisite zeal without sloshing the expensive paint from the can, pour half into another container. Stir the remaining half with a flat paddle, dredging the copper up from the bottom, until the bottom is clean and the copper is distributed throughout the paint. Still stirring, slowly pour the extracted portion back, mixing it in until all the paint is a uniform color and consistency.

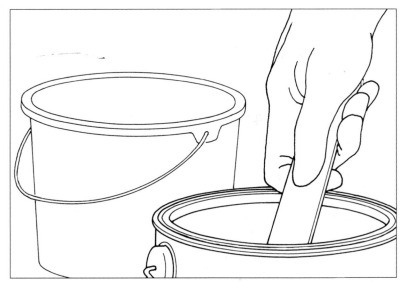

ROLLER APPLICATION

The easiest way to apply bottom paint is with a roller. Select a short-nap throw-away roller cover for this job. Use the paint as it comes from the can, without thinning. (On hot, windy days, some thinning may be necessary to get the paint to flow out.) An extension on the roller handle will keep you clear of droplets the roller may sling and will minimize the contortions required to paint hard-to-reach portions of the bottom.

For longer-lasting protection, apply two coats. This can usually be done in a continuous operation; i.e., by the time you finish rolling on the first coat, the paint in the area where you started will be dry enough to recoat. If you apply only one coat, at least give the hull a second coat at the waterline, where the scrubbing action of the surface tends to remove the paint more quickly.

Ablative paints—copolymers—require multiple coats to deliver satisfactory performance. It is a good idea to make the first coat a different color from the top coats. When the base-coat color begins to show, it will be time to repaint the bottom.

Mask the waterline or bootstripe before you begin. If you are painting bare gelcoat, wipe it thoroughly with a dewaxing solvent.

Pour a small amount of paint into the basin of the paint tray, stirring the paint each time you refill the tray. Roll the bottom paint onto the hull as quickly as you can. It is generally easier to roll up and down, that is, from waterline to keel. Save a bit of paint for the bottom of the keel and for the areas under the screw pads or wedges, to be applied when the boatyard workers relocate the poppets or when the boat is back in the slings.

TAPE

TRYING TO SAVE A COUPLE OF BUCKS by buying cheap masking tape is false economy. Almost any masking tape works fairly well when the paint is sprayed on, but when it is rolled or brushed on, the paint wicks under paper masking tape.

For crisp, sharp color separation, use *only* plastic "Fine Line" tape. Wider tape will tend to hold a straighter line. Save the paper tape for attaching masking paper to the hull—but not as a paint edge. Paper tape is also adequate to protecting surrounding fiberglass from varnish drops or runs.

Most masking tapes become difficult to remove with direct sun exposure of only a few hours, so remove the tape as soon as the paint is sufficiently dry to allow the tape to be peeled away without drawing out "strings" of paint. Peel masking tape by pulling it back on itself and slightly away from the painted edge.

RACING APPLICATION

Racing sailors may be concerned with the small paint ridges that sometimes form where the strokes overlap. These tiny ridges have no noticeable effect on normal boat performance, but for competition and for powerboat applications, rolling the paint from bow to stern may be preferable.

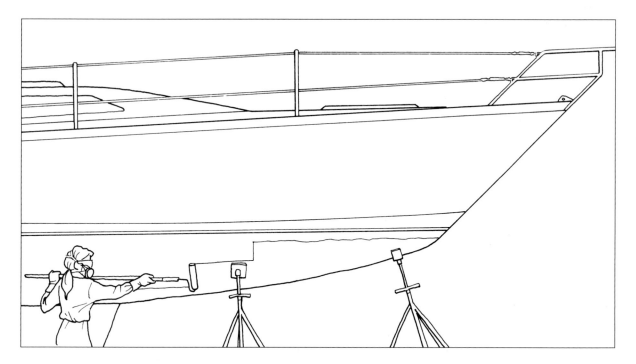

BURNISHING ANTIFOULING COATINGS

For an even smoother bottom, select a vinyl bottom paint, and after it is completely dry, burnish the surface with bronze wool or wet-sand it with 220-grit paper (or finer) on a foam block. Epoxy and copolymer bottom paints may also be burnished. For dry-stored boats, special buffable alkyd enamels are available. These have no antifouling properties and should be applied with the same roll/tip method recommended for topside enamels.

APPLYING CUPROUS RESIN

Bottom paints are, unfortunately, not environmentally friendly. Bottom coatings that do not leach out biocides into the water are available. While these seem to be effective against hard growth—barnacles, mussels, and the like—they are susceptible to the attachment of grass. These so-called permanent bottom coatings require periodic scrubbing (with a brush, not with a scraper) to keep them clean of grass, but if they last a number of years—test results are still early—periodic scrubbing may well represent less work and less expense than annual painting. An occasional brushing, not unlike washing your car, seems a small price to pay to eliminate the release of poisons into the water—and into the air and your lungs when sanding for a fresh application.

1 Permanent coatings are basically copper-loaded resins, either epoxy or vinylester. For application, the hull must first be stripped of all bottom paint. Even if your boat is decades old, expect the gelcoat to harbor traces of mold-release wax; wipe the bare gelcoat with a dewaxing solvent, turning and changing rags often. Sand the wax-free gelcoat lightly with 100-grit paper to smooth the surface and provide tooth for the coating.

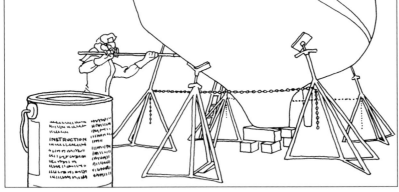

2 Apply the coating per the manufacturer's instructions, which usually involves rolling the resin on with a foam roller, perhaps smoothing the application with a foam brush. In the case of vinylester-based products, a wash coat of polyvinyl alcohol (PVA) may be required to seal the resin from the air.

3 When the resin is fully cured, remove the PVA with water and "activate" the coating— if required—by wet-abrading the surface with a scrubbing pad (Scotchbrite). If the boat is used seasonally, the cuprous resin coating will need to be activated each spring just before launch.

PROPS, ZINCS, AND TRANSDUCERS

Props may be left unpainted if the boat gets regular use; the rotation will keep the prop clean. If the boat sees less-frequent use, expect an unprotected prop to foul. Regular copper- or copper-oxide-based bottom paints will not stay on a bronze prop, and may contribute to galvanic action before they release. Special antifouling paints compatible with underwater metal are available, but they can require as many as four prime coats (eight hours apart) before two finish coats (24 hours apart). Most boatowners choose to simply polish the prop with emery cloth and give it a heavy application of wax, expecting to scrub the prop underwater if it fouls.

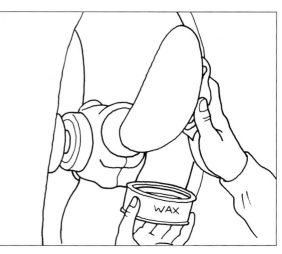

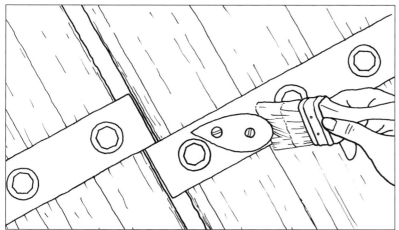

Underwater zinc anodes must never be painted. If they are removed when the bottom is painted, be careful not to paint any metal surface the mounted zinc will contact.

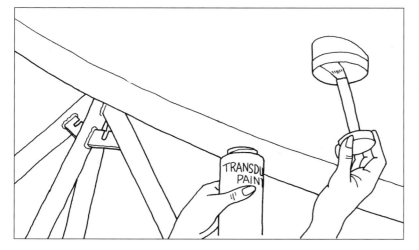

If not given an antifouling coating, depthsounder transducers will foul, causing false readings. The aggressive solvents in vinyls can attack the face of the transducer; other types are less likely to cause damage. If you are applying a vinyl bottom paint, protect the transducer with a primer coat of epoxy or apply a less aggressive paint (special transducer paints are available in small containers).

BOOTSTRIPE

The bootstripe is that narrow stripe of paint that separates the topsides from the bottom and gives your bottom paint a finished look. Usually black or an accent color, a bootstripe can be easily applied with bootstripe tape. This durable product is available in multi-stripe effects as well as a variety of widths and a rainbow of colors. Bootstripe tape is perfect for the slab sides of powerboats, but in order for the bootstripe to appear to have a uniform width on a sailboat, it must actually widen as the hull surface becomes less vertical. Conversely, uniform-width tape will appear to narrow where the hull is less vertical. If you want the width of the stripe to appear uniform, you will have to paint it.

FINDING THE WATERLINE

Check the waterline on a glass-calm morning. Be sure the trim of the boat is correct, redistributing equipment and supplies if necessary to get the correct bow attitude and eliminate any list. From the water or a dinghy, score the actual waterline on the hull at the bow and at both corners of the transom.

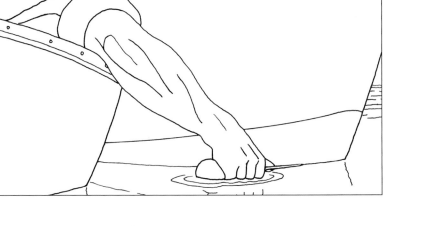

POSITIONING THE BOOTSTRIPE

1   If the existing bootstripe appears to be in the right location relative to the score marks, use it as the guide for your new stripe. If it needs to be raised or realigned, try to get the yard workers to level your boat to the score marks. You can make this easier by taking a carpenter's level aboard and finding two surfaces—one fore and aft, and one athwartship—that are level when the boat is floating on her waterline. If the yard blocks the boat up to make these two surfaces level, the three score marks will also be level.

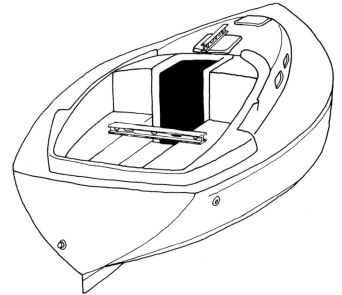

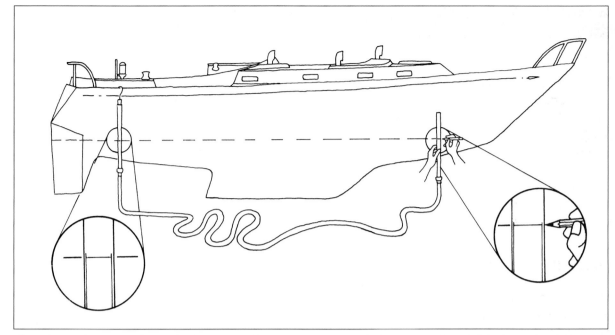

2 The modern way to locate the line joining the score marks is with a laser transit, but not all yards have this equipment. The poor man's solution is the water-filled hose. Put hose fittings (one male, one female) on the ends of a 3-foot section of clear $^3/_4$-inch vinyl hose, then cut the hose in half. Screw the pieces tightly to either end of a garden hose about half again as long as your waterline length. With wire or tape, hang one end from the rail with the bow score mark near the center of the clear section. Hang the other end with the top of the clear section at the stern score mark. Fill the hose from the high end until water runs out the low end. Now raise the low end 8 or 9 inches. The water level will remain even with the score mark, and if the boat is level, the water level at the other end will also be level with the score mark there.

You can walk around the boat with one end of the hose and mark as many points as you like for the waterline by holding the hose against the hull and making a pencil mark at the water level. Because the hose is flexible, the internal volume may vary, so a second person adding or spilling water as necessary to keep the level at the control point is recommended. Dewax the hull in the bootstripe area before you begin marking its location, then mark the hull every foot, more often if the hull is changing shape quickly.

3 Don't locate the bootstripe at the true waterline. It should be at least an inch above the water to prevent the stripe from fouling as a result of wave action or the boat being slightly out of trim. Mark the location of the stripe—bottom and top—at the control score mark, then add water to the hose to raise the level to these stripe locations. Use the other end of the hose to mark the hull all around. The stripe will vary in width, but the top will be a uniform distance higher than the bottom.

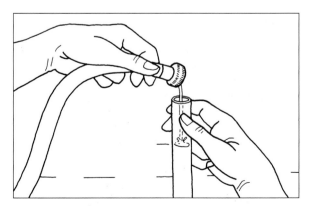

MASKING THE STRIPE

1 Use wide Fine Line tape to smoothly join the pencil marks on the hull. Tape above the lower-edge marks first to mask the top edge of the bottom paint. Let the bottom paint dry overnight.

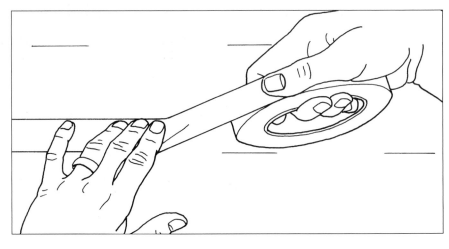

2 Apply a second strip of tape below and abutting the first strip, then remove the first strip.

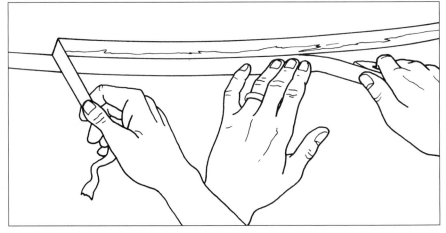

3 Apply a third strip above the upper-edge marks to mask the top edge of the bootstripe. Step away and check all taped lines for fairness; correct any hills or valleys. Burnish the inside edges of the tape with the bowl of a plastic spoon to press them tightly against the surface; this gives a sharper edge when you paint. Do not burnish the full width of the tape.

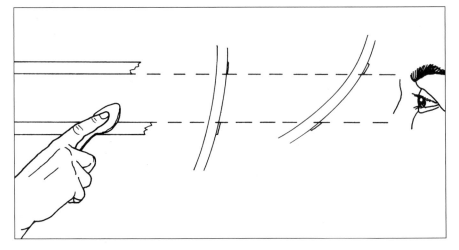

PAINTING THE BOOTSTRIPE

1 Sand the surface with 120-grit paper, taking care not to damage the edges of the tape. Wipe away all dust with a spirits-dampened cloth.

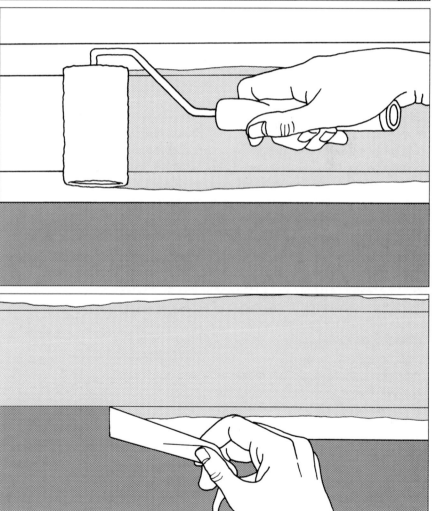

2 Cut a foam roller cover into sections slightly longer than the stripe width, and load a section onto a similarly shortened handle. (Handles with 3-inch roller cages are readily available.) Use alkyd enamel, one-part polyurethane, or bottom paint in a contrasting color. Apply it with your shortened roller, tipping it with a dry brush for a smoother finish, if you like. As soon as the paint is dry to the touch, apply a second coat. If paint is available, giving the stripe a third coat will extend its life.

3 When the paint is dry, remove the tape by pulling it slowly back on itself and slightly away from the painted surface.

ANTI-BLISTER COATING

Hull blistering—boat pox—is the fiberglass boatowner's anathema. A single blister brings dread more appropriate to the discovery of a subcutaneous lump under an arm. Fiberglass boats can die of boat pox, but it is exceedingly rare. Still, the discovery of blisters suggests some action should be taken. What may be appropriate is difficult to determine.

In the best case, a single blister or two can be treated like pimples, not pox. You can easily deal with such pimples yourself—see "Fairing and Minor Blister Repair." In the worst (repairable) case, the gelcoat and usually the first layer of laminate are precision peeled and replaced—usually with a sprayed mixture of vinylester and chopped-strand glass covered with a 20-mil barrier coat of filled epoxy. This is a process requiring specialized equipment and expertise, and the cost of this cure is likely to be around $300 per foot of boat length.

WHAT CAUSES BLISTERS?

Gelcoat, once thought to be impermeable, does in fact allow water molecules to penetrate. This wouldn't be such a big problem were it not for various water-soluble materials generally contained in the underlying laminates. These attract water like a dry sponge, setting up an osmotic flow through the gelcoat and potentially through the layers of laminate. As more water is absorbed, the "sponge" swells, causing internal pressures that become gelcoat blisters if the bond between the gelcoat and the first layer of laminate is weak. Because of layup procedures, the weakest bond is just as often between the first and second layers of fiberglass, meaning the blister will be located beneath the primary laminate. If you are wondering why the water under pressure doesn't just pass back out the way it got in, this is because the relatively small water molecules have combined with the water-soluble material into much larger molecules that cannot pass through the gelcoat.

Less than 20 percent of the time do blisters form deeper in the laminate than the first layer. This suggests that 80 percent of the time, blisters are a cosmetic rather than structural problem. This would be true except that the laminate may also contain water-soluble acids that, combined with water, can begin a chemical reaction that weakens the surrounding chemical bond.

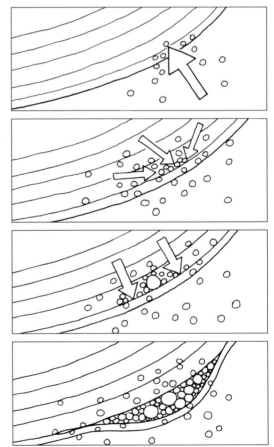

DETERMINING THE APPROPRIATE TREATMENT

What to do? If you have an older boat with no sign of blisters, the answer is do nothing. If you have a first-time blister, or a handful of blisters, the answer is to repair them and keep a close eye on the hull for further indication that a problem may be developing. If your hull has broken out with an undeniable case of pox, having the gelcoat peeled (and the first layer of laminate if the blisters are beneath it) may well be your only long-term solution. You could grind out and repair each blister, but the number of blisters suggests that the water that has penetrated the gelcoat is finding an ample supply of water-soluble materials in the laminate. That water is trapped inside the laminate, and can be dried out only by removing the gelcoat.

DRYING OUT

Of course, you may not want to do a $9,000 repair on a $6,000 boat. In that case, strip the hull of all bottom paint. Dewax the bare gelcoat. Locate, and grind open all the blisters. Scrub out the blisters with a warm TSP solution, then wash the entire hull with fresh water (hot if available). Let the hull dry for as long as possible. If you are planning to do this over a northern winter, tenting the boat will be essential. A catalytic heater in the tent can speed the process. Even in the South, the hull will need a couple of months out of the water if the humidity level is above 50 percent.

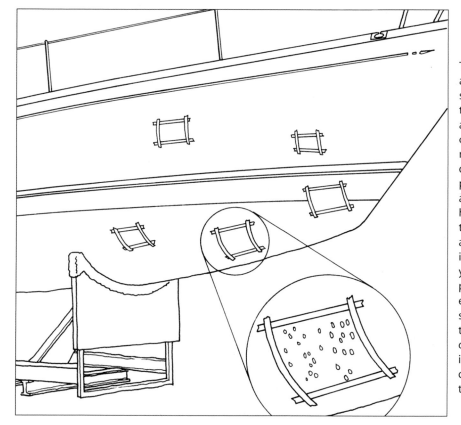

There are moisture meters around that supposedly measure the moisture content of the hull, but such readings are almost always suspect. A series of readings with the same meter might be useful for determining how the drying is progressing, but don't expect a moisture meter to tell you how wet your hull is (and don't take expensive corrective action based on such readings). The easiest way to check your hull is to tape squares of plastic—all edges sealed with electrical tape—over several spots on the hull, then check them after a couple of sunny days; if the inside of the plastic is damp, the hull needs more drying time. Dry the hull and the plastic and seal it back.

FILLING BLISTERS

Before apping an epoxy barrier coat to inhibit hull saturation, all existing blisters need to be ground open, drained, and scrubbed as detailed earlier. For more extensive instructions for repairing and preventing blisters, see *Sailboat Hull and Deck Repair* in this series.

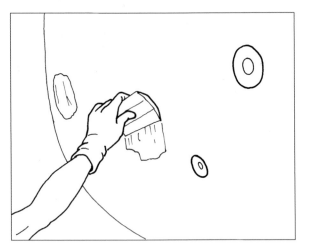

1 Paint the clean and dry depressions with an unfilled epoxy resin, such as West System #105, then thicken the same resin with collodial silica (West System #406) to a peanut-butter consistency and fill each of the ground depressions.

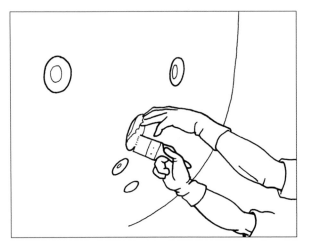

2 Deeper depressions should be laid up with epoxy-saturated layers of cloth (never use mat with epoxy). Fill the blisters flush with the surrounding hull surface.

3 When the epoxy has cured, scrub it with Scotchbrite and water to remove the surface amine.

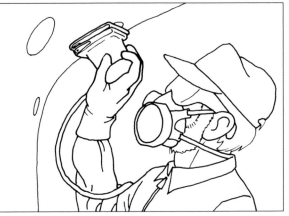

4 Fair all the blister repairs with the palm sander, and fill any voids with additional epoxy putty. Scrub and sand again to fair all repairs, then sand the entire bare hull with 80-grit paper. Wipe the surface clean with acetone or other recommended solvent.

APPLYING AN EPOXY BARRIER COAT

Barrier coatings are generally special formulations of epoxy resin that exhibit less permeability than gelcoat. The most effective formulations have microscopic flakes of impermeable material that act like roof shingles to prevent penetration. All barrier coatings depend on adequate thickness to work. A thickness of about 20 mils is generally specified by the manufacturer. Even if less is suggested, bringing the thickness up to 20 mils will improve the performance of the product.

Expect to apply a half-dozen coats or more of barrier coat to achieve the recommended dry film thickness (DFT). Use a foam roller to apply the barrier coating. Subsequent coats generally can be applied without sanding as long as you do not exceed the maximum recoat interval. To avoid weakening the barrier by sanding the coating, apply an epoxy-based bottom paint within a few hours of applying the last barrier coat—the coating manufacturer will provide exact times for varying curing conditions.

PROTECTING A NEW BOAT

SHOULD YOU PUT A preventive barrier coating on the hull of a new boat? The answer is no.

Applying a barrier coating requires sanding the gelcoat, which will automatically void the manufacturer's warranty. Don't even sand the bottom for that first coat of bottom paint without checking with the boat manufacturer; some require that you prepare the surface with "no-sand" etching process to avoid breaching the surface of the gelcoat.

Warranty issues aside, the negative impact of early blistering has led most boat manufacturers to review their hull construction. New materials are being used by many boat manufacturers that provide the same protection as a barrier coating. Some companies warrant their hulls for as long as 10 years against blistering. Wait until the warranty is nearly expired to add this extra level of protection.

TOPSIDES AND DECK

While gelcoat is much like paint, being polyester-resin based gives it an advantage as a boat surface: when the hull laminates are originally applied to the layer of gelcoat in the mold, the two form a strong chemical bond. This applies only to layup; the bond between a long-cured hull and gelcoat brushed or sprayed on to cover a ding or scratch is strictly mechanical—just like paint. (Wiping the surface with styrene just prior to coating *can* partially reactivate the old gelcoat and result in some chemical crosslinking, but as a practical matter this step is often omitted.)

Where gelcoat differs from paint is in its thickness. The recommended film thickness of paint is likely to be about 2 mils; the range for gelcoat is 15 to 20 mils. That makes it stand up to wear and abuse much longer than paint. Scratches are less visible since they don't cut through to some different color base. And the thick coating can tolerate repeated polishing to restore its gloss.

The main disadvantage of gelcoat is that it has poor flow characteristics. Its original gloss comes from being sprayed onto the highly polished surface of a mold. When it is applied like paint to an external surface, the result is a rough, irregular surface, a far cry from the incredibly smooth and glossy finish of, for example, polyurethane paint.

Still, when the surrounding gelcoat is in good condition, surface damage repairs should generally be made with gelcoat. Even though the gelcoat application may initially be rough, it can be sanded smooth and polished to blend imperceptibly with the rest of the hull.

GELCOAT REPAIR

Gelcoat is essentially polyester resin with pigment added. As such, it can be applied in much the same manner as polyester, used as a surface coating, or thickened into a filler.

OPENING A SCRATCH FOR REPAIR

A scratch typically cannot be successfully repaired by painting over it with gelcoat. The gelcoat is too thin to fill the scratch, and if it is thickened to make a gelcoat putty, the putty bridges the scratch rather than filling it. To get a permanent repair, draw the corner of a scraper down the scratch to open it and put a chamfer on both sides, then fill the groove with gelcoat putty.

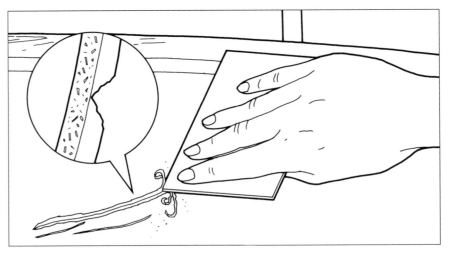

GOUGES AND OTHER DAMAGE REPAIRS

1 Damage to the underlying laminate must be repaired before applying the gelcoat. Shallow damage and drilled holes (where hardware has been removed) can be repaired with polyester resin thickened with chopped-strand glass. Epoxy resin must not be used for repairs that will be gelcoated because gelcoat does not adhere well to epoxy; stick with polyester resin for these repairs. Repair more extensive damage with a layer (or layers) of resin-saturated fiberglass fabric. "Fairing and Minor Blister Repair" in Chapter 4 provides more detail, but with polyester, use alternating layers of mat and cloth.

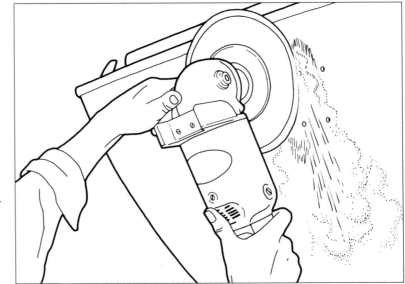

2 Use a polyester fairing compound—you can make your own by adding microballoons to the resin—to fair the repair prior to gelcoating.

3 Be sure the finished repair is below the surface or grind it below the surface with a disk sander and 100-grit paper. Otherwise you will cut through the new gelcoat when you later attempt to sand it flush with the surrounding surface. Vacuum or brush away all dust and loose fibers, and wipe the area thoroughly with acetone.

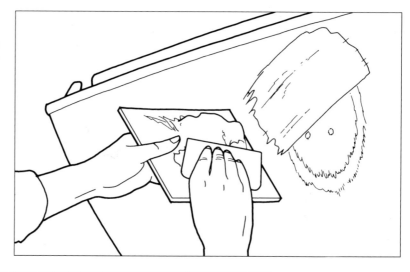

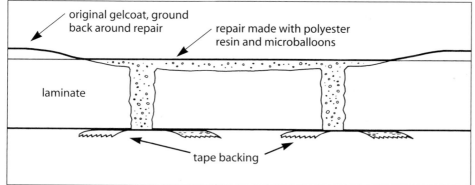

original gelcoat, ground back around repair

repair made with polyester resin and microballoons

laminate

tape backing

GELCOAT CHOICES

You will find gelcoat available as both a resin and in a thicker putty form called paste. The paste is what you want if you are repairing a scratch; repair kits containing a small amount of gelcoat paste and hardener along with a selection of pigments can be purchased for less than $20. For larger areas choose plain gelcoat, sold by the quart. You will also need coloring agents to tint it to the color you need.

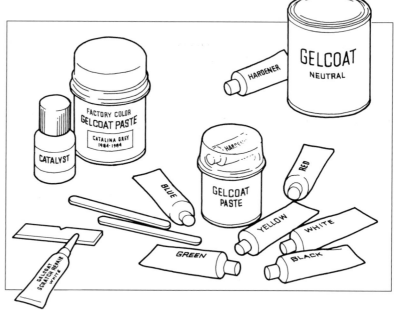

COLOR MATCHING

Gelcoat is also available in "factory" colors, but you are likely to have a difficult time finding one that is a perfect match for a hull that has been exposed to the fading rays of the sun for a few years. You will do as well buying pigments and tinting the gelcoat yourself.

1 What colors do you need? Go to a paint store and find a color-sample card close to the color of your hull. Show the card to the store clerk and ask what the formula is—the store custom mixes this color by adding pigments to a white base. If he tells you the mix calls for four units of blue and one of yellow, you need blue and yellow tints—and white. Sometimes the formula will call for half a dozen different tints. At least half of those, the ones called for in the least amount, are added to tweak the color to just the right shade. For gelcoat matching, the two or three primary tints should get you close enough.

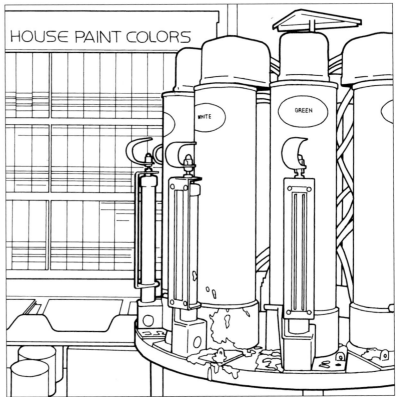

2 Be sure the coloring agents you buy are intended for use with polyester resin. Start with exactly 1 ounce of gelcoat, and add pigment a drop at a time, stirring between drops. Keep track of the number of drops. When the color looks close in the cup, put a drop of the mix on the gelcoat for a better comparison, then make any needed adjustments. When you're satisfied—don't expect perfection—write down the per-ounce formula to get the right color. Always tint the resin *before* you add the hardener.

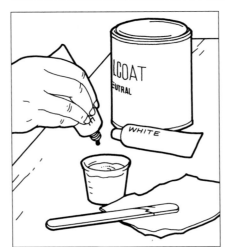
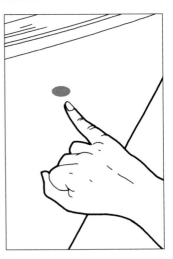

CATALYZING

The hardener for gelcoat is the same as for any polyester resin—methyl ethyl ketone peroxide, or MEKP. Most gelcoat will require one to two percent of hardener (by volume). As a general rule, four drops of hardener will catalyze 1 ounce of resin at one percent.

Follow the manufacturer's instructions for catalyzing the gelcoat. It should not kick in less than 30 minutes. Hardening in about two hours is probably ideal, but overnight is just as good unless the wait will hold you up. Always err on the side of too little hardener. Also be certain to stir in the hardener thoroughly; if you fail to catalyze every bit of the resin, parts of the repair will be undercured.

SPREADING GELCOAT PASTE

Gelcoat paste is applied like any other putty—with a plastic spreader. If you are filling a crack, the putty may bulge a little behind the spreader. This is okay: polyester resin shrinks slightly as it cures, and you are going to sand the patch anyway. Just don't let it bulge too much or you'll make extra work for yourself. Scrape up any excess beyond the patch area.

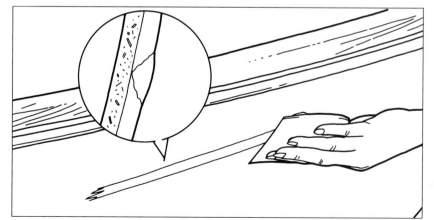

APPLYING GELCOAT WITH SPRAY

You can apply gelcoat over larger areas by brush, roller, or spray. Spraying can give the best initial finish, but it is also the most demanding way of applying the gelcoat. Gelcoat applied by brush or roller is likely to need a bit more sanding to achieve a polishable surface, but in the end you will be unable to determine how the gelcoat was applied. If you are comfortable spraying it on, do it that way; otherwise use a brush or a foam roller.

Getting gelcoat through a sprayer nozzle requires thinning the resin with styrene or toluene. Use a small gun with light to medium air pressure. If you don't have a spray gun, you can still spray the gelcoat with a Preval-type sprayer that uses a can of compressed air as the propellant. These are available for under $5.

Mask around the repair area to avoid getting gelcoat on any surrounding surfaces. Spray on the gelcoat with long, overlapping strokes. When the surface is coated, immediately apply a second coat with a spray pattern running diagonally across the first. Because the thinner flashes off very quickly, the gelcoat should show no tendency to run or sag with immediate recoating. Follow the second coat with a third one applied in another direction. Three sprayed coats should give you a skin thickness of about 15 mils. Giving the surface a fourth coat will give you extra gelcoat to work with—not a bad idea if this is your first experience with it.

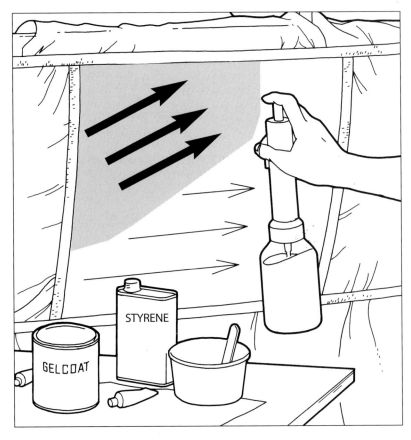

COVERING THE REPAIR

GELCOAT WILL NOT FULLY CURE in air. Regardless of how you apply the gelcoat, coat it with polyvinyl alcohol by brushing or spraying the PVA on after the gelcoat kicks.

APPLYING GELCOAT WITH BRUSH

For brush application, use the tinted and catalyzed gelcoat without thinning.

Because the gelcoat in the cup and the gelcoat on the surface are curing at about the same speed, you can't wait for the first application to kick and then apply a second layer without mixing up fresh gelcoat. The solution to this if the layer is too thin is to add a thickening agent to the gelcoat so that the first application is 20 mils thick. The usual thickening agent for gelcoat is dehydrated talcum, available in small quantities from your resin supplier. Add only enough to give a test stroke a 20-mil thickness. Be sure your test stroke doesn't exhibit a tendency to sag; if it does, stiffen the mixture by adding more thickener.

1 Lay the resin on in steady, slow strokes, much like a finish coat of varnish.

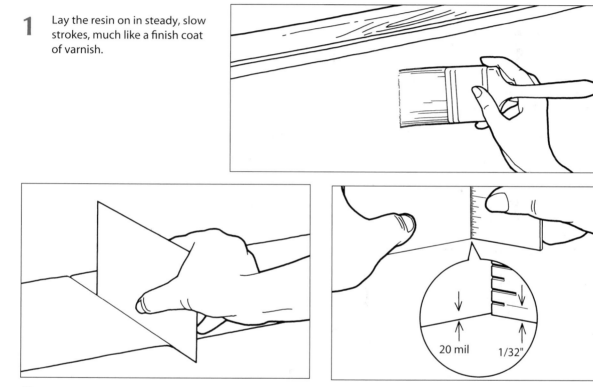

2 Check the thickness by "slicing" the test stroke with the edge of a piece of paper and comparing the height of the gelcoat on the paper to a 1/32" mark on a ruler, which is about 30 mils.

APPLYING GELCOAT WITH ROLLER

Roller application of gelcoat can give a more uniform thickness and a smoother surface. As with brush application, some thickening may be required to achieve the appropriate thickness with a single application. Use a foam roller cover cut to the appropriate width for the repair. Make a test application to check the thickness and thicken as necessary. Apply the gelcoat to the surface with a well-saturated roller, rolling in two directions.

SANDING AND POLISHING GELCOAT REPAIRS

Wash off the PVA—it comes off with just water. The amount of sanding required depends on how smoothly you applied the gelcoat. If the gelcoat is a perfect spray application, light wet sanding may be all that is required, but for purposes of instruction, let's assume your repair resembles discarded chewing gum. Skip the steps your own repair doesn't require.

1 It is possible to use a power sander to remove a lot of extra gelcoat, but this requires great caution. A much safer approach to a lumpy gelcoat patch is to do the initial sanding with 120- or 150-grit paper on a sanding block. Use short strokes, taking care that the paper is sanding only the patch and not the surrounding surface. Keep in mind that the hull shape is probably convex in the repair area, so don't sand the gelcoat flat.

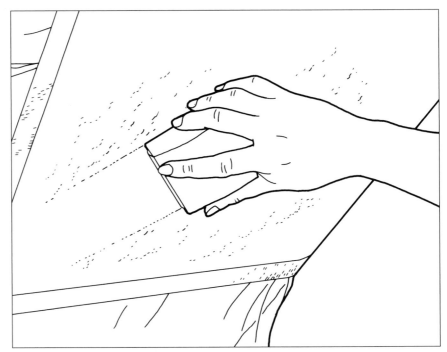

2 For a scratch repair, the edge of a 5½-inch length of 1 x 2 makes a convenient sanding block. Never do this initial sanding without a block backing the paper.

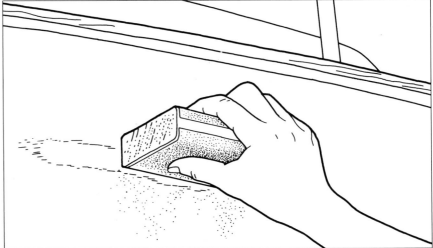

220

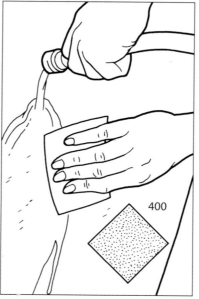

400

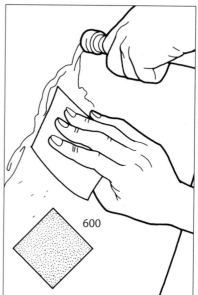

600

3 When the new gelcoat is flush, put 220-grit wet-or-dry paper on your block and wet sand the repair, feathering it into the old gelcoat until you can detect no ridge with your fingertips.

Switch to 400-grit wet-or-dry, abandoning the block, and wet sand the surface until it has a uniform appearance.

Follow this with 600-grit wet-or-dry.

4 Dry the area and use a buffing compound to give the gelcoat a high gloss. On small repairs, you can buff the gelcoat up to a gloss by hand. If the area is large, or if you want to buff the entire hull, buy or rent an orbital polisher. Either way, the process is the same. Apply the buffing compound to the surface, then buff it with a circular motion, using heavy pressure at first, then progressively less pressure until the surface is glassy. If your color match is reasonably good, the repair will be virtually undetectable.

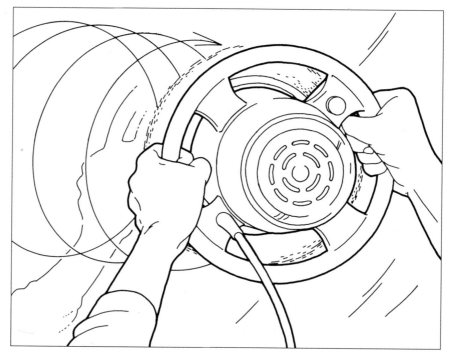

TWO-PART LINEAR POLYURETHANE

There may be valid reasons to use enamel or single-part polyurethanes (which are actually modified enamels) to paint the deck of a boat, but there is not a single reason to use anything but two-part linear polyurethane on a fiberglass hull. On deck, the limited working time the two-part paint affords can cause problems as you try to paint around hardware, portholes, or sections of nonskid, but the uninterrupted expanse of the hull is the ideal surface for applying polyurethane. The appearance and durability of two-part polyurethane is likely to be worth the extra effort of removing hardware and carefully mapping the sequence of application to use it on the deck, but electing to follow an easier course also has merit. However, the fact that two-part polyurethane is not appreciably more difficult to apply to an uninterrupted surface than any other paint makes all other choices for refinishing the hull significantly inferior.

PREPARING THE SURFACE

If your hull is in good condition, all that is required to prepare it for painting is dewaxing and sanding. A heat gun will make short work of removing any registration numbers or other vinyl graphics or stripes, but be sure not to heat the fiberglass enough to damage it. If it's too hot to touch, it's too hot. If the hull has been previously painted or is wood or metal, a conversion coat or a special primer will be required; follow the paint manufacturer's instructions.

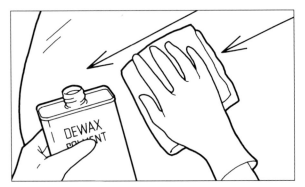

1 No matter how old it is, every fiberglass hull must be solvent-wiped to remove all traces of wax, silicone, or mold-release agents. Dewax before sanding or the sandpaper will drag the wax into the scratches, making it far more difficult to remove. Soak your cloth with dewaxing solvent and wipe the hull in a single direction, as though sweeping a surface clear of sawdust. Turn the cloth often, and change it when you run out of fresh sides; otherwise you will spread the wax rather than remove it.

2 Sand the entire hull with 120-grit paper. If you will be sanding away the old bootstripe (a good idea), be sure to score the hull before you start so you can locate the waterline later.

CHECKING FOR POROSITY

Two-part polyurethane paints can be applied directly onto fiberglass in good condition. However, by the time most hulls need to be painted, the gelcoat has developed some porosity that will cause the paint to crater. Check the surface for porosity by applying paint of any kind—bootstripe enamel is perfect—to a test area on the hull. Examine the paint carefully for any sign of cratering, then wipe it from the hull with a solvent-soaked cloth. The paint may also form "fish eyes" (you'll know one when you see it), which indicate you need to do a better job of removing wax or silicone from the hull.

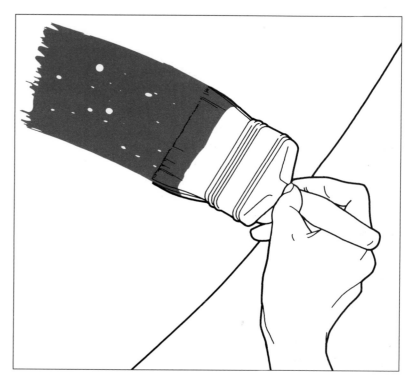

SURFACE CRAZING

In addition to porosity, old gelcoat may exhibit crazing—a pattern of tiny cracks in the surface similar to a cracked eggshell. Don't confuse surface crazing, which usually appears over a wide expanse, with stress crack associated with hardware mounting or molded corners. See *Sailboat Hull and Deck Repair* in the International Marine Sailboat Library for stress-crack repair.

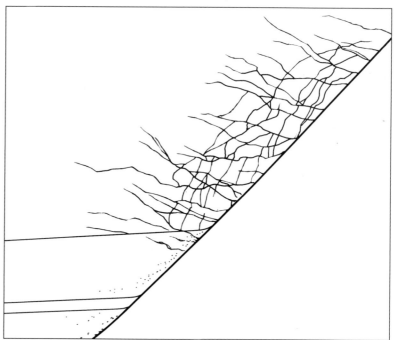

EPOXY PRIMER

The solution for both porosity and surface crazing is the same—a coat or two of epoxy primer. You may also need to apply epoxy primer as a conversion coating if the fiberglass has been previously painted. Check for compatability by wetting a cloth with the thinner for your linear polyurethane and taping it against the painted surface (in an inconspicuous spot) for about 10 minutes. If it softens or lifts the old paint, a conversion coating is required. Follow the instructions from the polyurethane manufacturer.

1 Mix the epoxy primer according to the label instructions and roll it onto the hull with a foam roller, without fuss. Allow it to cure overnight, and sand the surface with 120-grit paper. One coat will generally be adequate to correct porosity, but a second prime coat may be required for crazing.

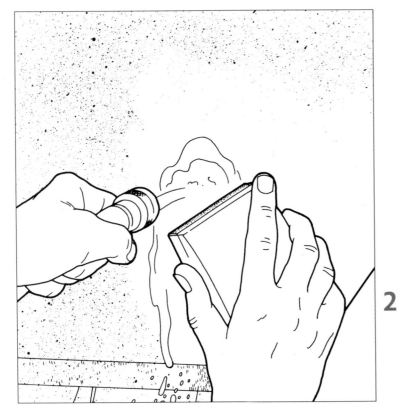

TIP: Often it is very hard to see where you have sanded, especially on a white hull on a bright day. The solution to this is to *lightly* mist the surface with a can of dark **spray lacquer** (light on a dark hull). The lacquer dries instantly, and it comes away easily as you sand, making the sanded areas distinct from those not sanded. The spray pattern will also help prevent your eyes from losing focus on the otherwise featureless expanse of hull—a common and disconcerting occurrence.

2 Surface flaws that the primer obviously will not cover can be filled with fairing compound. After the first prime coat, apply this creamy epoxy filler to each spot with a small spreader. It will be dry enough to block sand in a few minutes. The second prime coat should give you a flawless surface.

SPRAYING POLYURETHANE PAINT

WHEN APPLIED BY BRUSH OR ROLLER, polyurethane paint is hardly more hazardous than oil-based enamel, but atomize polyurethane with a paint sprayer and it becomes potentially lethal. A component of this paint is isocyanate. If that sounds to you like it might be related to cyanide, you're paying attention. In aerosol form, this stuff is poison—pure and simple. Spraying polyurethane without an air-supplied respirator is not just foolhardy, it is stupid. You can get as good a finish—often better—by rolling and tipping this amazing paint, but if you are set on having your boat sprayed with polyurethane, don't be *dead* set on it. Pay to have it done by a professional with the required safety equipment.

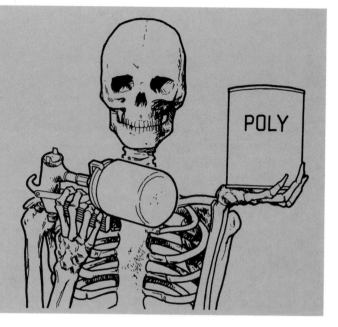

MIXING AND THINNING POLYURETHANE PAINT

1 Mixing two-part paint is straightforward—put the designated amount of part A into the desired amount of part B and stir.

2 Thinning is not so well defined, and getting just the right amount of thinner in the paint is the key to getting a perfect finish. The trick is to sneak up on proper mix. The paint manufacturer's recommended ratio is no more than a starting point. In cool, dry weather, you will need less thinner; in hot, humid weather, more. Start with slightly less than called for and test the paint for flow.

TESTING FLOW-OUT

A scrap piece of window glass provides a perfectly smooth test surface for determining the flow characteristics of your mix. Set the glass vertically, and paint an area, using a throw-away brush and vertical strokes. Tip the test horizontally with your good brush. If the brush strokes fail to disappear entirely in a couple of minutes, you need more thinner. Add a capful to your mix and test again. Keep thinning a capful at a time until the brush strokes just disappear. If the paint runs or sags, you've added too much. Recover by adding a couple of additional ounces of paint to the mix. (Set a little mixed paint aside just for this purpose.) When the paint seems right, pour some into your tray, and roll and tip a test spot on the glass to make sure it is right for the film thickness you will be getting from the roller.

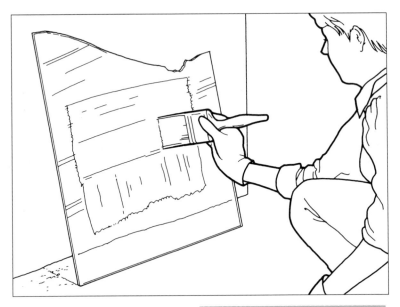

TIP: Getting the thinner right is the only difficult part to using two-part paint. You can greatly improve the likelihood of a perfect finish on your boat if you get familiar with the paint by first painting a dinghy or other small surface. Otherwise, paint just the transom of your boat first, mixing only enough paint for this limited area. Learning errors will be easy to sand out.

ROLLING POLYURETHANE (LIGHT COLORS ONLY)

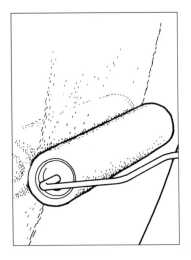

If you are applying white polyurethane (or any light color), you can get a very nice finish without ever touching a brush to the hull. Simply roll the paint on the hull with a solvent-resistant foam roller, taking care not to let the ends of the roller leave tracks. The rolled-on paint will dry to a high gloss with a very slight orange-peel texture, similar to a just-less-than-perfect spray finish. This is the easiest way to apply polyurethane, and you should try a test surface (the transom, for example) before deciding to roll and tip a light color. Dark colors will not flow out as well and require tipping with a brush.

KEEPING THE SURFACE CLEAN

THE WET GLOSS FINISH OF polyurethane will not only emphasize every underlying surface flaw, it will show dust contamination like a pimple on Elle MacPherson's face. Just before mixing the paint, always thoroughly wipe the surface you plan to paint with a solvent-dampened cloth, following with a clean, dry cloth.

The quick-skinning nature of two-part polyurethanes make them less susceptible to airborne dust contamination. Nevertheless, wetting the ground all around the boat with a mist spray from a garden-hose nozzle before you paint will help hold down dust that might otherwise find its way to the wet surface of your paint or into your paint tray.

THE ROLL-AND-TIP METHOD (ALL COLORS)

Done properly, tipping rolled-on polyurethane with a "dry" brush results in a finish that can only be described as stunning. Although one person can both roll and tip, the process is far easier with less opportunity for disaster if two people are involved.

Beginning at one end of the hull, the roller applies a uniform coat of paint to an 18- to 24-inch section of the hull, depending on the freeboard. If the freeboard is such that a roller load of paint will not cover at least 18 linear inches of the hull, you will have to apply the paint in over-and-under blocks, working with two wet edges.

The tipper follows behind the roller with a top-quality (badger or ox-hair) brush, tipping the surface of the paint lightly with a series of deliberate, parallel strokes toward the new wet edge. The tipper begins each stroke well back, gently "landing" the brush just behind the old wet edge and drawing it just beyond the new wet edge (see "'Laying

On' the Finish Coats" in the varnish section). The tipper's brush is never dipped in paint except that already applied to the hull.

While the last application is being tipped, the roller reloads the foam roller from the tray, rolling out all excess. When the tipper is finished, the roller is ready to coat the next section of the hull, just overlapping the wet edge. The tipper follows. Tip/load. Roll. Tip/load. Roll. Continue the process without pause or hesitation from one end of the hull to the other.

It is possible to continue right on around the bow or stern to the other side, painting the hull in one continuous session, but this is rarely done because one side of the hull is likely to be in the sun, and painting in the sun inhibits the flow of the paint. If you are continuing around to the other side, pause long enough to let the tipper clean his brush in solvent and dry it.

Painting with two-part paint is a sprint. Never go back and try to brush out a flaw; you will only make it worse. All problems with the first coat can be sanded out before the top coat is applied. With two people working together, expect the job to take less than a minute per foot. If it is taking you longer than that, your pace is too slow.

WET SANDING BETWEEN COATS

Let the first coat dry overnight, then wet sand it with 340-grit wet-or-dry paper. Never wet sand with an electric sander. However, to make the sanding go much faster, you can use a finishing sander on a surface moistened with water from a trigger sprayer if you are very careful to keep the moisture out of the tool. Thick rubber gloves are recommended as a precaution—as good as this finish will be, it's not to die for. Sand out any sags, runs, or other surface flaws. This is another good time to mist the surface with a contrasting spray of lacquer.

REMOVING SANDING SCUM

Sanding urethane produces a scum that is more tenacious than ordinary sanding dust. Flush the sanded hull with water, scrubbing as necessary. When the surface is dry, wipe it with a solvent-dampened cloth.

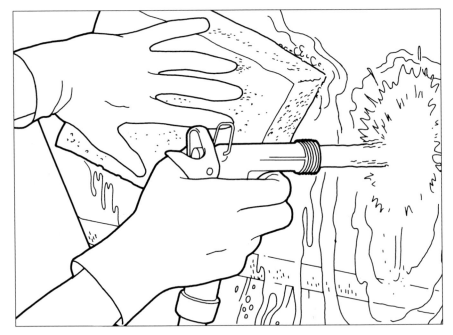

GETTING A MIRROR FINISH

The only thing different about the second coat is that you now know exactly what should and shouldn't happen. Thin the paint carefully to get it exactly right, then lay it on the hull in a nearly continuous flow. The results will be spectacular.

Two coats are generally adequate, but if you are dissatisfied with the results of your second coat, the cost of a third coat is nominal, and you begin it with twice the experience level you had on the previous coat. Stop at three—you aren't likely to get better. Besides, the improvement will be so dramatic that no one but you will ever notice the little flaws. Soon enough you won't notice them either.

COVE STRIPE

MOST FIBERGLASS HULLS HAVE A MOLDED-IN indentation for a cove stripe. Like the bootstripe, a cove stripe can be painted on or applied with tape. Regardless of how you intend to renew this stripe, you must strip and clean the indentation at the same time you are preparing the rest of the hull—before applying any primer or paint.

The molded-in recess generally simplifies painting. Mask the stripe with Fine Line tape laid to the edge of the recess. Use boottop enamel, and apply two or three coats with a brush. Two-part polyurethane is not a good choice for cove-stripe paint because it tends to wick under the masking tape. If the edge of the indentation is sharp, you may get as good or better results painting the stripe freehand, using a solvent-dampened rag as you go to clean away any paint that gets outside the recess.

The uniform width of a cove stripe makes it well suited for a tape application rather than paint. Stripe tape is available in myriad colors and widths from both marine chandleries and automotive stores. It is a simple matter to apply the tape, trimming the ends to match the recess contour. Solvent-wipe the recess before applying stripe tape.

Using an alkyd enamel or a single-part polyurethane on the deck will give you more time to work the paint around obstacles and still tip the paint out to a flawless finish. Your ability to get a perfect finish on deck with two-part polyurethane will be vastly improved if you remove as much deck-mounted hardware (including handrails) as practical. The extra work is repaid by the longer life of the polyurethane. Actually, removing hardware before painting will improve the job no matter what paint you choose because it eliminates edges where paint failure begins—the paint extends under the hardware. Besides, if the deck needs painting, the hardware likely needs rebedding anyway.

DEALING WITH NONSKID

Fiberglass decks generally have a pattern of molded-in nonskid. Painting nonskid surfaces reduces their effectiveness. To offset this effect, use a nonskid additive on those areas of the deck, even if the molded-in pattern is deep and well defined.

You may also want the nonskid portions of the deck a different color from the rest of the deck. In either case, refinishing the deck usually requires painting the smooth portions of the deck separately from the textured portions.

Paint the smooth surfaces first—for two reasons. First, the smooth surfaces are usually painted white, the nonskid a color; color covers white better than the other way around. Second, if the final masking between the two is done on the textured surface, it will be hard to get a sharp line between the two.

SURFACE PREPARATION

Preparing the smooth portions of the deck for paint is identical to preparing the hull. The textured nonskid sections require a little different approach.

1 Use terry cloth—sections of old bath towels—to dewax the non-skid. The rough surface of the terry cloth penetrates the craggy nonskid.

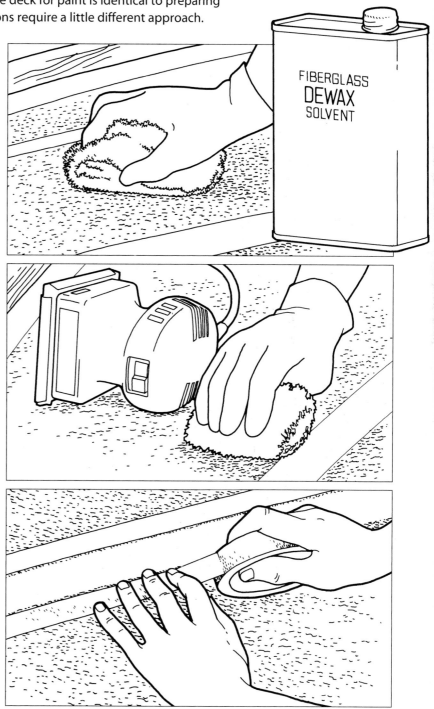

2 Sanding the bottom surfaces of the nonskid is not possible, but abrade the surface with coarse bronze wool, using short, quick strokes. Fortunately most of the stress on the new paint will be on the top surface, which you can sand. Machine sand the nonskid surface with 120-grit paper. Scrub the surface thoroughly with a brush and a hose, and let the surface dry completely before proceeding.

3 Mask all nonskid surfaces, applying the tape just inside the mold line. If the gelcoat is porous or crazed, remember to use an epoxy primer before applying the finish paint.

LIMITING WET EDGES TO ONE

1 Where the smooth part of the deck branches to divide or encircle sections of nonskid, you will find yourself dealing with two wet edges. If the branch branches again, you have three, maybe even four wet edges. And so on. Dealing with more than one wet edge is sure disaster with polyurethane and likely to cause problems with any kind of paint.

2 Avoid this by "mapping" the deck into manageable sections and masking off branches. For example, you might mask off all athwartship sections, then paint the deck between the nonskid and the rail all the way around the boat. When that is dry, move the tape to the other side of the paint lines (i.e., mask the section just painted) and paint the athwartship sections individually. Lines between sections will hardly be noticeable—a feature of the deck—and you avoid the disastrous problems of multiple wet edges.

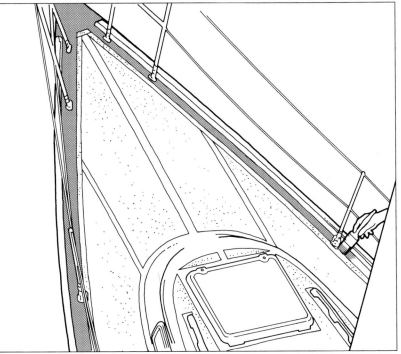

PAINTING MOLDED NONSKID SURFACES

1 After the smooth surfaces are dry, mask them and paint the nonskid sections. Instead of a foam roller cover, one with a longer nap may do a better job of getting paint into the bottom of the molded pattern. Give the new coating nonskid characteristics by introducing grit into the paint. This can be done in two ways.

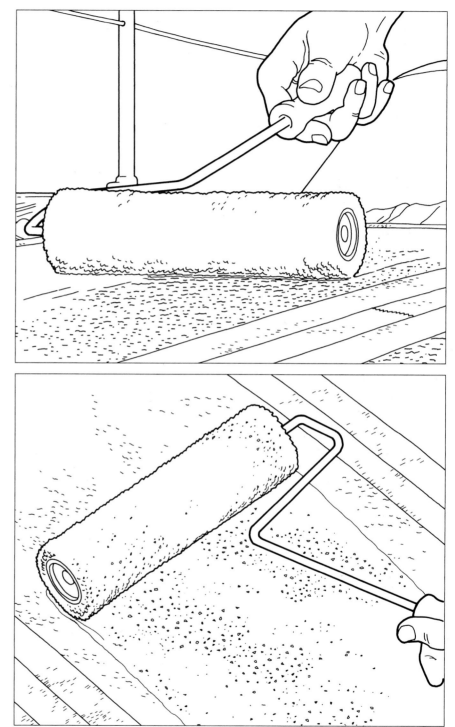

2 Paint manufacturers generally offer a nonskid additive—usually polymer beads—to be mixed into the paint before you apply it. Adding grit to the paint is easy and gives the rolled coating—there is no reason to tip paint on nonskid surfaces—a rough texture. Unfortunately the beads settle almost immediately to the bottom of the paint tray, resulting in irregular dispersion of the grit on the painted surface.

3 An alternative method providing a more aesthetically pleasing result is to first coat the nonskid area with an epoxy primer, and while the epoxy is wet, cover the entire surface with grit sifted from your fingers or a large shaker.

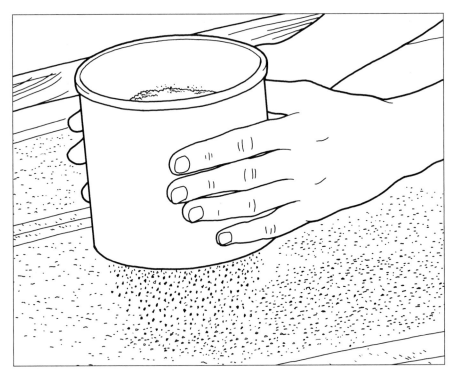

4 When the epoxy kicks, gently sweep off the grit that didn't adhere (you can use it on another nonskid area), and encapsulate the grit that remains with two rolled-on coats of paint. This results in a nonskid finish that few will find unattractive.

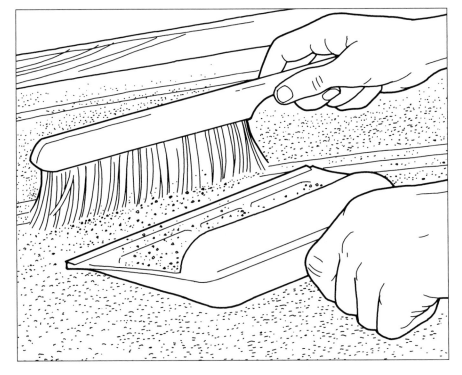

NONSKID OVERLAY

For the best footing, you might want to consider a rubberized nonskid overlay, such as Treadmaster M or Vetus deck covering. These are far more expensive than paint, but they do enhance security, and they can improve the boat's appearance as well, hiding old, worn-out nonskid textures. If you will be applying overlay, carry the paint ½ inch into the nonskid area when you paint the deck.

PREPARING THE SURFACE

Before the overlay can be applied, any molded-in texture must be removed. Most of the texture can be quickly taken off with a disk sander and a 36-grit disk. (A belt sander can also be used.) Be careful not to let the sander get outside the textured area. It is neither necessary nor desirable to grind away all the pattern. Fill the remaining depressions with epoxy putty. When the epoxy cures, sand the surface to fair it and prepare it for the adhesive.

CUTTING PATTERNS

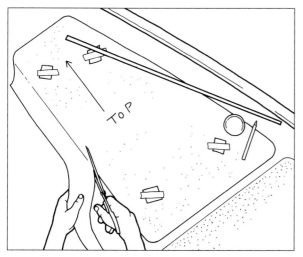

1 Make a pattern from heavy kraft paper for each of the nonskid panels. Cut the paper oversize, then place it on deck to trace the exact outline. Tape across holes cut in the center of the paper to hold it in place. Use a flexible batten to draw curved edges, a can lid for uniform corners. For appearance and drainage, leave at least 1 inch between adjacent panels, at least twice that between the nonskid and rails, coamings, or cabin sides. Write TOP on the pattern to avoid confusion when you cut the overlay, and draw a line on it parallel to the centerline of the boat, with an arrow toward the bow.

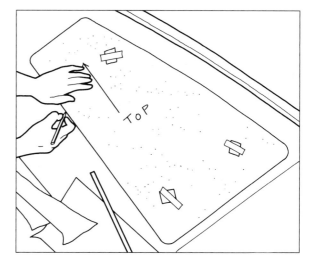

2 Do not cut patterns for only one side, expecting to reverse them for the opposite panels. Boats are almost never symmetrical, and hardware is certain to be in different locations. Cut a separate pattern for every panel. When all the patterns have been cut, tape them all in place and evaluate the overall effect before proceeding. Trace around each pattern with a pencil to outline the deck area to be coated with adhesive.

CUTTING THE OVERLAY

1 Place the patterns top-side down on the back of the overlay material. Depending on the overlay you have chosen, it may be necessary to align the patterns; use the line you drew on each pattern for this purpose, aligning it parallel to the long edge of the sheet of material.

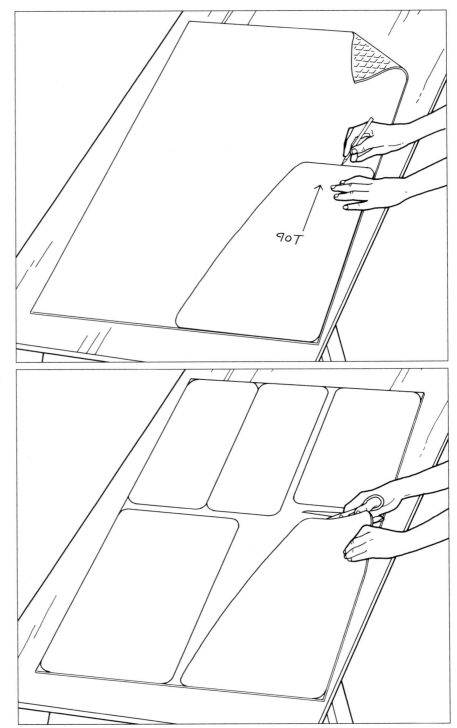

2 Position all the patterns on your material to minimize the waste before making any cuts. Trace each pattern onto the overlay, then cut out the pieces with tin snips or heavy scissors.

APPLYING THE OVERLAY

If the overlay manufacturer doesn't specify a different adhesive, glue the non-skid to the deck with thickened epoxy.

1 Coat both the outlined deck area and the back of the nonskid with the adhesive, using a serrated trowel.

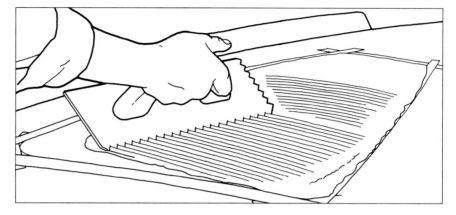

2 Position the nonskid on the deck and press it flat, beginning with pressure in the middle and working outward to all edges.

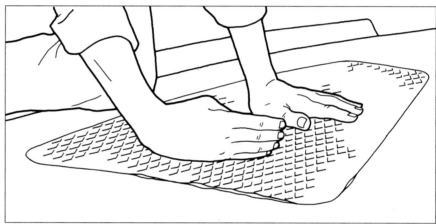

3 Pick up any squeeze-out with a putty knife, and clean away the residue with an acetone-dampened cloth. Continue applying each section in turn until all are installed.

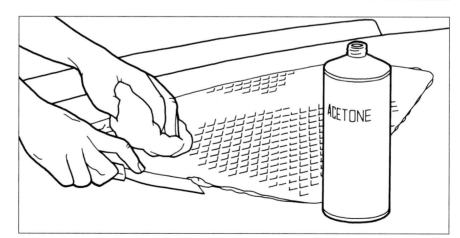

FINISHING TOUCHES

Masts used to come out of the boat every year to be checked for splits and rot, then get a fresh coat or two of varnish in the spring before being re-stepped. Today most masts are extruded aluminum, anodized against corrosion, and they may remain upright for a decade or more without *any* maintenance other than checking points of attachment for spreaders, tangs, and other hardware. That doesn't mean they don't show their age: A mast that has seen a decade or two of service is usually streaked with oxide and crosshatched with halyard scars. With fresh gloss on hull and deck, now is the time to spruce up that stick.

Your refinishing also can't be considered complete until the boat's name is back on the stern or the quarter. Unless you were satisfied with stick-on block letters, this used to be the domain of the professional signpainter. No more. With inexpensive computer-generated graphics, you can apply the name in virtually any configuration imaginable. And if your taste runs to eye-catching hull graphics, you have reached the fun part.

A couple of decades ago traditional wood rubrails began to be replaced with aluminum, then with vinyl. Aluminum and vinyl promised lower maintenance than wood, but, after a few years of exposure and a few encounters with fixed objects, aluminum rails typically look scarred and shabby, and vinyl rails harden, break, and fall off. It is possible to partially restore an aluminum rail by polishing it if it isn't badly damaged, but vinyl rails must be replaced. This can be a major undertaking if the boat manufacturer is out of business. Fortunately vinyl extrusions are used for thousands of other applications, so take a piece of your rail to a plastic extrusion supplier and you are likely to find something that will work and complement your new paint.

By the time a fiberglass boat needs refinishing, the plastic windows, especially the fixed deadlights in the main cabin, are likely to be fogged or crazed. Although not strictly refinishing, replacing portlights makes a striking difference in a boat's appearance. Detailed instructions for their replacement can be found in *Sailboat Hull and Deck Repair* in the International Marine Sailboat Library.

The final touch should be bright, new canvas—sailcovers, a dodger, cockpit cushions. Find the instructions to make all these items and many others in the *Canvaswork and Sail Repair* volume.

REFINISHING THE MAST

Having a mast reanodized is fairly expensive, not to mention the difficulty of getting a long spar to the treatment facility. Painting is justifiably the more popular solution. Forget about trying to protect your mast by spraying it with some kind of clear coat; by fall your deck will be aflutter with cellophane leaves. The best coating for your mast is the same as for your hull—two-part polyurethane.

1 Support the unstepped mast on sawhorses and remove as much hardware as you can. Wipe the mast with a cloth soaked in acetone or other solvent recommended by the paint manufacturer. Sand the entire mast with medium-grit emery cloth to remove oxidation and to give tooth to the surface of the mast.

In order to allow the uninterrupted coating of the full circumference, suspend the mast above the horses with supports in the ends of the mast and metal rods through mounting holes in the center. The sail track should be facing up. Rewipe the suspended mast with solvent.

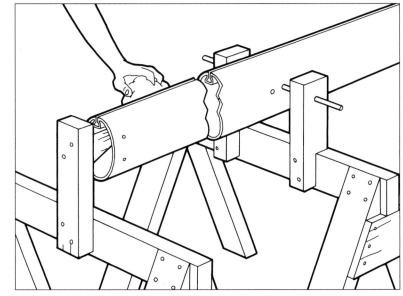

2 The key to a long-lasting finish is the prime coat. The specified undercoat for aluminum will probably be an acid-type primer that etches the metal to provide a better grip for the paint. Apply the primer per label instructions. Spray or roll it on to avoid introducing brush strokes. Acid primers are not sanded.

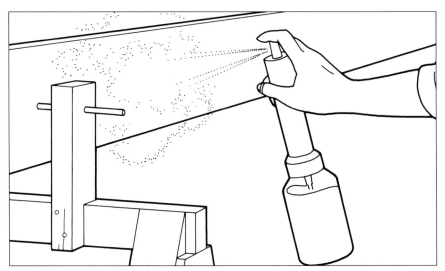

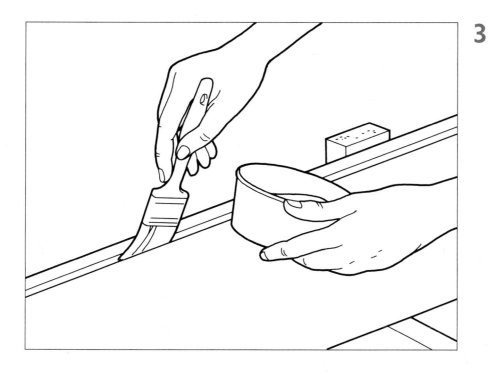

3 The most popular color for the finish coat is white, but black and buff are also common. Of course, you can paint your mast any color you like. Whatever the color, apply the urethane with a roller. Tipping is not likely to be necessary. Let the first finish coat dry overnight, and wet sand it with 340-grit paper before applying the top coat.

You will need a brush to cut the paint around any hardware you failed to remove and to get paint into the sail track.

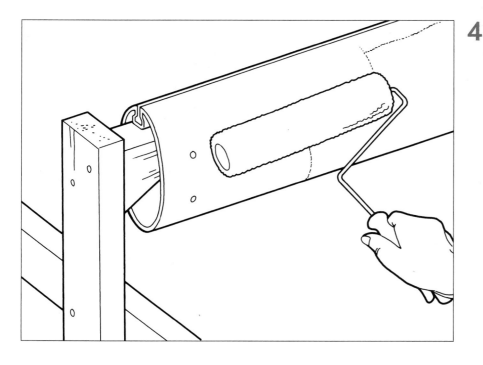

4 Start at the top end of the mast, painting 2 feet of the track with the brush, then running the lightly loaded roller all around the mast to coat the surface. Paint the mast in 2-foot sections, maintaining a single encircling wet edge. If you have problems early on, don't fret; they will be well out of sight, and by the time you get to the deck end of the mast, you will have found a rhythm and technique that gives you the quality finish you want.

GRAPHICS

It isn't that difficult to do a workman-like job of painting the name on your boat with spray mask, an X-acto knife, and can of spray enamel. One color. Block letters. Ho hum.

For a little more money and a lot less work, you can kick some stern. There seems to be no limit to what is now possible with computer-generated boat graphics. A graphics supplier can convert your most imaginative idea for your transom into an electronic image—allowing you to evaluate it on a computer screen and make appropriate modifications—then give it to you as a vinyl appliqué contoured and sized to precisely fit your boat. For the hull sides, eye-catching graphics in a rainbow of colors can be created and applied with similar ease.

DESIGNING CUSTOM GRAPHICS

For a boat name, the designer will provide you with examples of available fonts, examples of special effects—outline, shadow, arch, etc.—and a selection of solid and metallic colors. All you have to do is measure the area where the name will be applied and determine curvature of the hull—the designer will tell you exactly how. Hull curvature will affect how the applied graphic appears and must be accounted for to get the appearance you envision. You also pick a font, a letter size, a style, and a color or colors. A local supplier can show you the combined effect of your selections on a computer monitor and make instant alterations until you are satisfied. A distant supplier will send or fax a printed image for your approval.

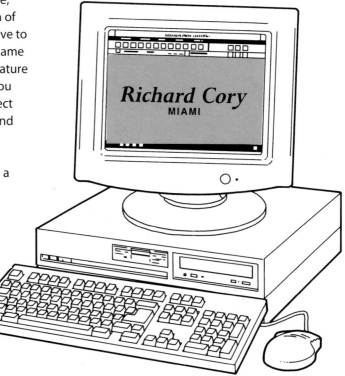

For custom graphics, you will need to work directly with the designer.

LAYING OUT VINYL GRAPHICS

When you receive the appliqué, it will come as a single sheet to allow you to position it properly on the hull. The sheet will have both a centerline and a baseline printed on it.

Begin the layout by cleaning the area of the hull where the graphic will be applied. Locate the center-line of the area; on the stern, for example, measure from side to side. Draw the center-line on the hull with a pencil, making sure the line is long enough to extend beyond the appliqué at both the top and the bottom.

Position the graphic on the centerline and move it up and down until you locate the

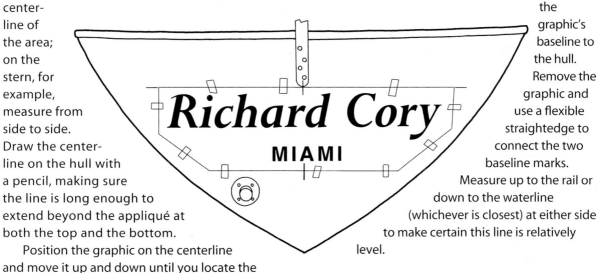

right position. Tape it in place and step back from the boat to evaluate the location. You may need to ascend a stepladder to get the proper on-the-water perspective. If a hailing port will be included, now is also the time to position it.

Once you are satisfied with the location, transfer the graphic's baseline to the hull. Remove the graphic and use a flexible straightedge to connect the two baseline marks. Measure up to the rail or down to the waterline (whichever is closest) at either side to make certain this line is relatively level.

DEALING WITH A LARGE APPLIQUÉ

One you have it aligned, you may find it easier to work with a sizable graphic if you cut it into smaller pieces. The actual decal is sandwiched between the decal backing and a transparent sheet of application tape. Make your cuts between words or letters. If you make these cuts in a gentle S-curve rather than straight, the pieces will only fit together one way when put on the hull. The alternative is to put a couple of inch-long horizontal alignment marks on the back of the tape where you will be cutting the graphic, then cut them in half when you scissor the appliqué.

APPLYING VINYL GRAPHICS

1 *Never* try to apply vinyl graphics on a windy day. Remember the last time you tore off a 3-inch strip of cellophane tape and it immediately folded back on itself? Once you peel away the backing from your decal, you are dealing with a sheet of sticky-faced tape measured not in inches but in square feet. If the wind flips one corner back on itself, either your boat will have a shorter name or you will be paying for a new graphic. Even on a still day, an extra pair of hands will cut down on adrenaline production.

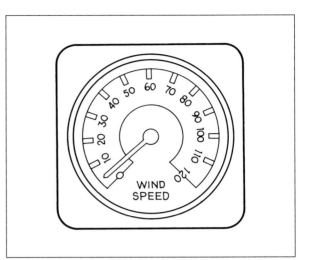

2 Put the graphic on a flat surface, tape-side down, and carefully peel the paper backing. If the decal starts to come away with the backing, use a knife to gently separate the two, then hold the graphic against the tape with the flat of the blade while you continue peeling the backing. If you are applying the graphic in sections, peel the backing from the center section first.

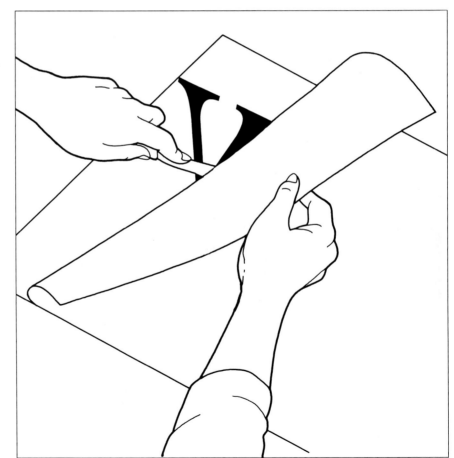

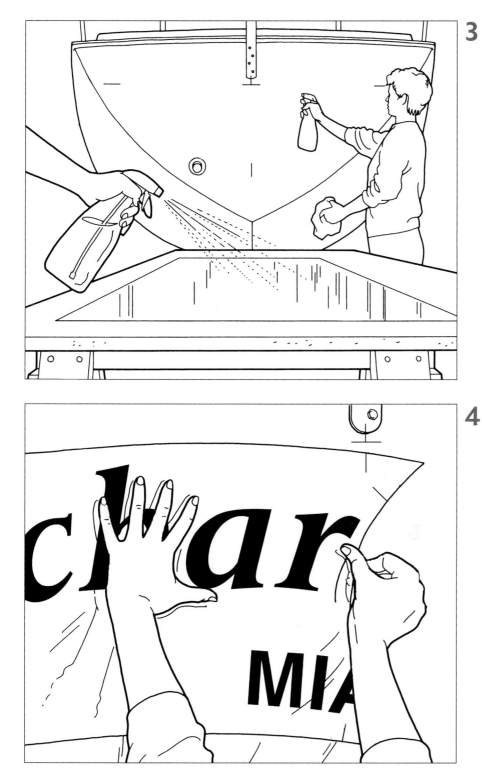

3 Spray the adhesive side of the graphic with window cleaner (Windex). Also spray the hull where the graphic goes, using a cleaner-soaked sponge to make sure the entire surface is wet. Be careful not to wash off your alignment marks.

4 Position the decal on the hull. The window cleaner allows you to slide the decal into the exact position—aligned with both the centerline and the baseline—but try to get close to start.

5 Making sure the graphic doesn't move, squeeze the moisture out from under it with a plastic squeegee. Start at the center and work toward the edges. If the graphic is in pieces, apply each piece in turn, working out from the center piece. Give the decal's adhesive at least 15 minutes to grab the hull—longer if the weather is cold—before the next step.

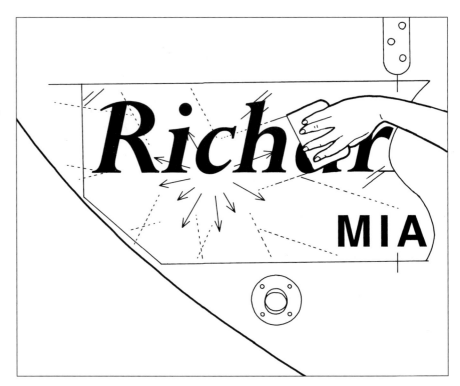

6 Spray the application tape heavily with the window cleaner, then use the squeegee with heavy pressure on the wet application tape to rub down the letters and graphics against the hull.

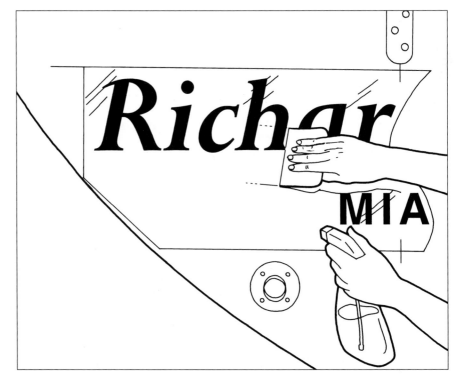

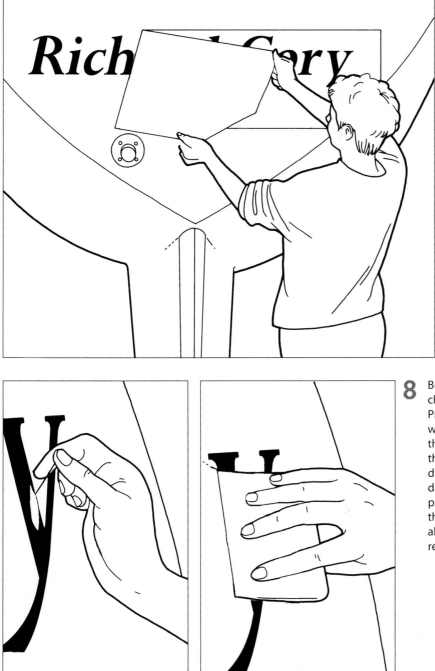

7 *Slowly* peel away the application tape. If the decal shows any tendency to come up with the tape, stop; you haven't waited long enough. Smooth the tape back down, rerub the lifted section of decal, and wait another 10 or 15 minutes before removing the tape.

8 Burnish the installed decal with a cloth to remove any trapped air. Prick any bubbles at one edge with a pin to let the air escape, then burnish the bubble flat with the squeegee. (Small bubbles will disappear on their own in a few days.) Now back away. Could a pro have done any better? Give the decal a day to set, then wash all the alignment marks and glue residue off with soapy water.

That's it. There is just one thing left to do. Wad up those paint-stained coveralls and don your sailing hat. It's time to paint a wake on the bay.

INDEX

Acetone, properties and uses, 20, 35, 100, 108, 127
Ajax cleanser, 64
Alcohol, denatured, 71
Alkyd enamel, 45, 91
    properties and uses, 9, 97, 120
Aluminum, painting of, 130–31
Anodes, zinc, 93
Appliqués, vinyl, 4, 133–37
    See also Graphics

Barrier coatings, 101
Bilges, 45
Bleach, for surface cleaning, 35, 64, 67, 72–73
Blisters, 98–101
    cause of, 98
    determining treatment of, 99
    drying out hull with, 99
    fairing, 100
    filling, 100
    repairing minor, 87–89
Block, sanding, 28
Boat pox, 98
Bootstripe
    dewaxing, 95
    masking, 90, 96
    painting, 97
    positioning, 94–95
Bootstripe tape, 94
Boottop enamel, properties and uses, 10
Borax, 73
Bottom
    blisters, 87–89
    brushing, 92
    painting, 83–101

preparing, 84
pressure washing, 84
sandblasting, 85
sanding, 85
scraping, 84
stripping, 86
Bottom paint
    ablative, 90
    antifouling, 83, 91
    applying, 90
    copolymer, 16, 90
    epoxy, 15
    mixing, 89
    racing enamel, 17, 91
    soft, 17
    thin-film Teflon, 17
    tin-based, 17
    vinyl, 16
    zinc oxide, 17
Bristles. *See under* Brushes
Bronze wool, 71, 80, 91
Brush cleaner, 87
Brush comb, 24
Brushes
    badger-hair, 23, 79, 117
    bristle types, 23
    China, 23
    chisel-trim, 23
    cleaning, 24
    foam, 23
    hog, 23
    Jen polyfoam, 23
    natural, 23
    ox-hair, 23, 79, 117
    quality of, 22, 23
    selecting, 23

synthetic, 23
width, 23
wrapping, 25
Brushing techniques, 49–50, 51, 77, 109
Brush spinner, 24, 25
Bulkheads, 45, 53
    color of, 53
Bungs, 33
Burnishing, antifouling coatings, 91
    cabinet scrapers, 31

Cabin, 45–62
Cabinets, 53
CAD/CAM, 4
Canvas, 129
Canvaswork and Sail Repair, 129
Caps, 32
Catalyzing, 107
Checking old paint, 36–37
Chisel, 33
Cleaning, surface, 35, 42
Cleats, removing, 34
Comb, brush, 24
Computer assisted design/manufacturing, 4
Contact cement
    applying, 58
    properties and uses, 18, 58
Copolymer bottom paint, properties and uses, 16
Cores, of roller covers, 25
Corian, 53
Costs, 4
    of paints, 9–21
    of strippers, 21, 39
Counters

replacing old surfaces, 55–60
replacing trim, 61
Coveralls, 32
Cove stripe, 119
Crazing, 113
Cuprous resin, properties and uses, 17

Decks
nonskid. *See* Nonskid surfaces
refinishing, 120–27
Degreasing, surface, 35
Depthsounder transducers, 93
Detergent, for surface cleaning, 35, 64, 67
Dewaxing, 36, 92, 95, 112
Diaper rash cream, 9
Dressings, 68
Drill, electric, 28
Dry film thickness (DFT), 101
Drywall knife, 33, 55, 57
Dust
cleaning, 42, 43
preventing, 78, 116

Edges, paint, 34
Emery cloth, 27
Epoxy
barrier coating, 101
bottom paint, properties and uses, 15, 91
filler, 100
primer, 114, 124
properties and uses, 15, 127

Fairing, 41, 87, 100, 105
Fairing compound, polyester, 105
Ferrule, of a brush, 22
Fiberglass, for repairs, 88, 104
Files, 31, 54, 60
Filters, for paint, 47, 76
Fine Line tape, 90, 96
"Fish eyes," 113
Flow characteristics, 4, 8, 48
Formica, 53–61
Fouling protection, 5, 8, 83

Gelcoat, 8, 33, 36, 38, 72, 88, 101
blisters, 98. *See also under* Blisters
dewaxing, 92
hardener for, 107
kinds of, 105
porosity, 113
properties and uses, 18
rolling, 109
sandblasting, 85
sanding, 41, 110–11

strippers effect on, 70, 86
surface repairs with, 103
vs. paint, 103
waterlogged, 83, 98
Gelcoat repairs, 88–89, 104–11
brushing, 109
catalyzing, 107
color matching, 106
crazing, 113
gouges, 104–5
polishing, 110–11
sanding, 110–11
scratches, 104
spraying, 108
thinning, 108
Gloves, 32
Goggles, 32
Graphics, 4, 129, 132
applying, 134–37
burnishing, 137
laying out, 133
Grit, of sandpaper, 27, 39–40

Handrails, removing, 34
Hardware, removing, 33, 120
Heater, for drying, 99
Hull graphics. *See* Graphics
Hydrochloric acid, 65

Keel, painting, 90

Lacquer, spray, 114
Lacquer thinner, 71
Laminate. *See* Plastic laminate
Laser transit, 95
Lemon oil, properties and uses, 12, 45, 67
Linear polyurethane, 11
Linseed oil, properties and uses, 12, 66
Lockers, 45

Magazines, boating, 8, 9
Magi-Sol, 86
Mahogany, 63, 69
Marine alkyd enamel, 10
Mask, dust, 32
Masts, 129
color for, 131
refinishing, 130–31
MEK, properties and uses, 20, 35
Melamine, painting over, 52
Methylene chloride, 38, 39, 72, 86
Methyl ethyl ketone peroxide (MEKP), 107
Microballoons, 105
Microfibers, 100
Mildew, 66, 67

Mineral spirits, properties and uses, 20, 42, 66, 67, 68, 75
Moisture meter, 99

Name, lettering for, 129, 132
Nap, of roller, 25
N-methyl-2-pyrolidone, 39
Nonskid overlay, 125–29
applying, 127
cutting, 126
patterns for, 125
preparing surface of, 125
Nonskid surfaces, 120–24
epoxy primer for, 124
grit for, 123–24
"mapping," 122
masking, 122
overlay. *See* Nonskid overlay
painting molded, 123–24
preparation of, 121
wet edges of, 122

Oil stone, 31
Orbital polisher, 111
Osmotic flow, 98
Oxalic acid, 64, 72

Paint
ablative, 16
antifouling, 9, 17, 28, 30, 91
bottom, 4–5
brands of, 8–9
cans, 46–47
compatibility, 36
copper-based, 5
filters for, 47
guide to, 9–21
keeping fresh, 52
local knowledge of, 9
non-ablative, 15, 16
old, 36–37
pouring, 46–47
quality of, 4
selecting, 8
skin on, 47
thinning, 48
types, 9–21
Painting techniques, 49–50
Peel Away, 86
Phenolic core, 25
Plastic laminate
checking adhesion, 55
cutting, 57
gluing, 58
installing new, 53–61
paper patterns for, 56

preparing for painting, 52
removing the separator, 59
rolling, 59
Plug, brush, 22
Polyester, 104
Polymer beads, 123
Polysulfide sealant, properties and uses, 19
Polyurethane
    single-part. *See* Single-part polyurethane
    two-part. *See* Two-part polyurethane
Polyurethane sealant, properties and uses, 19
Polyurethane varnish, properties and uses, 14, 45
Polyvinyl alcohol (PVA), 92, 108, 109
Portholes, servicing, 34
Portlights, replacing, 34, 129
Preparation, 33–43
Pressure wash, 84
Preval sprayer, 108
Primer
    acid-type, 130
    epoxy, 114, 124
Propellers, 93

Quality, of paint, 4

Racing, 91
Rags, 32
Resin
    cuprous, 17, 92
    epoxy, 100, 104
    laminating, 88
    melamine, 52
    polyester, 88–89, 104, 106
Respirator, 32, 58, 85
Roller, using, 51, 90, 97, 109
Roller covers, 25
    cutting, 26
Roller handles, cage-type, 26
Router, 54
    for trimming, 60
Rubrails, 129

Saber saw, 54, 57
Safety, equipment for, 32
    with contact cement, 58
    with methylene chloride, 72
    with polyurethane, 32, 43, 115
    with sanders, 40, 85
    with strippers, 38, 39, 72, 86
Sailboat Hull and Deck Repair, 113, 129
Sandblasting, fiberglass, 85
Sanders

block, 28, 41
disk, 28, 39, 55
finishing, 29
orbital, 29
palm, 29, 40, 100
random-orbit, 29, 39
Sanding, 39–41, 74
    hand, 41
    laminate, 55
    varnish, 77
    wet, 40
Sandpaper
    folding for hand-sanding, 29
    types and uses, 27, 39–41, 111
Scotchbrite, 92, 100
Scrapers, paint, 30, 69, 70
    sharpening, 31
Screw pads, painting, 90
Scrubbing pads, 92
Sealants
    polysulfide, 19
    polyurethane, 19
    silicone, 19
Sealers, 68
Silicone, removing, 36
Silicone sealant, properties and uses, 19
Single-part polyurethane, properties and uses, 11, 52, 97, 120
Soft-bottom paint, properties and uses, 17
Spar varnish, properties and uses, 14, 45, 68, 69
Spritzer bottle, 78
Stanchion bases, removing, 34
Stress cracks, 113
Stripper
    chemical, 21
    peel-type, 86
    "safe," 39, 86
    using, 38
Sun-screening agents, 4, 8, 69, 81

Tack rag, 78
Tape, masking, 90
Teak, 63
    cleaning, 64, 65
    oiling, 64, 66
    sanding, 74
    sealers, properties and uses, 13, 68
Tenting, 99
Thin-film Teflon, properties and uses, 17
Thinner, for cleaning, 24, 42
    lacquer, 71
    reusing, 25
    types of, 21
    using, 48

with varnish, 75
Thinning, paint, 48
Tin-based paints, 4–5
    properties and uses, 17
Tin snips, 54
"Tipping," 51
Toluene, properties and uses, 21
Tools, 22–32
    keeping fresh, 52
    laminate work, 54
    quality of, 22
Tooth, 40
Topside enamel, properties and uses, 10
Topsides, 103–19
Transducers, 93
Treadmaster M, 125
"Treatments," for teak, 68
Trim, removing, 33–34
    replacing, 61
Trisodium phosphate (TSP), 35, 64, 88
Tung oil, properties and uses, 13, 66
Turpentine, 66, 75
Two-part polyurethane
    benefits of, 112, 130
    hazards of, 115
    keeping clean, 116
    mirror finish on, 119
    porosity for, 113
    preparing surface for, 112
    properties and uses, 11, 45, 112–19, 130–31
    roll-and-tip application of, 117
    rolling, 116, 131
    sanding scum from, 118
    spraying, 115
    testing flow of, 116
    thinning, 115
    wet sanding, 118

Ultraviolet inhibitors, 69, 81
Urethane-modified alkyd, 11
Urethane varnish. *See* Polyurethane varnish, properties and uses

Varnish
    bubbles, 76
    clouding, 75
    maintaining, 81
    polyurethane, 14
    quality of, 4
    sanding, 77
    scratches in, 81
    selecting, 69
    spar, 14, 45, 68, 69
    stripping, 69–71
    using, 45, 49, 69–81

weather's effect on, 75
    when to use, 75
Varnishing
    finish coats, 79
    initial coats, 75–78
    preparation, 69, 74
Vetus deck covering, 125
Vinyl bottom paint, 16

Water
    for cleaning dust, 43
    for wetting down, 43
Waterline, finding, 94–95
Waxes, removing, 36
West System #105 epoxy, 100
West System #403 microfibers, 100
Wet edges, 122
Windex, 135
Windows, plastic, 129
Wood finishes, 63–71
Wows, 41

Zinc anodes, 93
Zinc oxide, 9, 17

The *McGraw·Hill* Companies

1 2 3 4 5 6 7 8 9 DOC DOC 0 9 8 7

Library of Congress has cataloged the cloth edition as follows:
Casey, Don
    Sailboat refinishing / Don Casey.
        p.   cm. — (The International Marine sailboat library)
  ISBN 0-07-013225-9
    1. Sailboats—Maintenance and repair—Amateurs' manuals. 2. Finishes and finishing—
Amateurs' manuals. I. Title. II. Series
  VM351.C33 1995
  623.8'223'0288—dc20   95-31120
                                                 CIP

Paperback ISBN-13: 978-0-07-148658-3
Paperback ISBN-10: 0-07-148658-5

Questions regarding the content of this book should be addressed to

International Marine
P.O. Box 220
Camden, ME 04843
www.internationalmarine.com

Questions regarding the ordering of this book should be addressed to

The McGraw-Hill Companies
Customer Service Department
P.O. Box 547
Blacklick, OH 43004
Retail customers: 1-800-262-4729
Bookstores: 1-800-722-4726

Illustrations in Chapter 1 (excluding the opener and page 34) by Paul Mirto
Illustrations in Chapters 2 and 4 by Rob Groves
Illustrations in Chapters 3, 5, and 6 , plus Chapter 1 opener, and page 34 by Jim Sollers